Published by WRL Publishing
Dallas, TX 75214
USA
wrlpublishing@gmail.com

THE INVISIBLE KING

EXPOSING HAWAI'I'S HISTORY
Conspiracy, Invasion,
Overthrow & Illegal Occupation

and now...
RESTORING A NATION

ALIE JAMES

Copyright © 2015-2016 by Alie James

All rights reserved. This book or any portion thereof may not be reproduced or used in any manner whatsoever without the express written permission of the publisher except for the use of brief quotations in a book review.

You Always Believed

You Always Believed
that Hawai'i is the 50th State of the United States,
But You Were Purposely Deceived,
with a Revised Story of Historical Events.

"Each time a man [or woman] stands up for an ideal, or acts to improve the lot of others, or strikes out against injustice, he sends forth a tiny ripple of hope, and crossing each other from a million different centers of energy and daring those ripples build a current which can sweep down the mightiest walls of oppression and resistance."

Robert F. Kennedy

Martin Luther King, Rosa Parks, Russell Means, Mahatma Gandhi, Nelson Mandela, Dalai Lama and Aung San Suu Kyi. These are people who fearlessly faced opposition, and struck out against the injustices of the day with peaceful resistance. The list of unnamed people, who came before and after these men and women, is beyond measure. For their cause, most of them suffered greatly.

But the One who suffered as no other has many names. I call him, Jesus Christ. He is the greatest example of what it means to suffer on behalf of others. He has taught me that it is essential to stand up against oppression and injustice, with unconditional love.

Love (Aloha) is the source of all selfless acts of courage, and is the creative force that allows the greatest good of all of life, to manifest.

Throughout my life, I've challenged myself to find the greatest good and truth in the things I'm most passionate about. One, is knowing completely who God is, and the other, is standing up for a cause that is noble, and worthy of my attention. Knowing His Royal Majesty through his writings gave me a deep appreciation and affection for his work and love for Almighty God. I've never known a more humble and brilliant man, who has sacrificed everything to restore his beloved nation - The Kingdom of Hawai'i. I am ever humbled by his humility, grace and love - for his Kingdom and for mankind.

May the world come to know his love as I have, through the writings that only a King blessed of God, could produce.

Alie James

Dedication

This book is dedicated to the King's Mother Cecelia Ku'ulei Silva and the King's daughter, Princess Collette Maile Silva. These two beautiful women are with us in Spirit, and continue to watch over and inspire the restoration of the Kingdom of Hawai'i. Their deep love and sacrifice for the King and the Kingdom have greatly influenced the man that King Edmund Keli'i Silva Jr. has become, and their Spirits continue to inspire him as he forges the Path of Aloha for all of us – in Hawai'i, and throughout our planet. I especially want to give thanks to the Queen Mother, as she is the one, who in a moment of divine inspiration, suggested the King write a book. It is because of her, that I myself was inspired to write it. This book is also dedicated to the King's father, Edmund Keli'i Silva, Sr., who continues to guide and support him. His love for the King and his family, greatly contributes to the King's tireless effort to move the nation forward.

The King's Mother
Cecelia Ku'ulei Silva

Princess Collette Maile Silva
King Edmund Keli'i Silva, Jr.

The King's Father & Mother
Edmund Keli'i Silva, Sr.
Cecilia Ku'ulei Silva

TABLE OF CONTENTS

Dedication iii
Book Cover Pictures.. ix
Preface xiii
Introduction 1
Part 1 Proof of Queen Lili'uokalani's Illegal Overthrow................... 6
   The Overthrow of the Kingdom of Hawai'i.................................. 6
      In 1893, On the Beautiful Island of Oahu.............................. 6
   Admission of Guilt - Public Law 103-150 8
      "Whereas" Statements are the Preamble to Legislation 8
      "Whereas" Statements of Public Law 103-150 9
   The Treaty of Annexation 21
      Queen Lili'uokalani Protests Against Annexation................... 21
      The Hawaiian People Protest Against Annexation 26
      Despite the Protest of the Queen & the Hawaiian People........ 27
   The Undeniable, Indisputable Truth 28
      The Kingdom of Hawai'i Is Due Full Restoration 28
Part 2 Story Details... 30
   Forgiveness and the Aloha Spirit.. 30
      Should the Nations of the World Be Forgiven?...................... 30
      Going Forward, Ignorance is Not Acceptable......................... 31
   Two American Presidents Agree 32
      President Grover Cleveland 32
      President Bill Clinton 33
      President Grover Cleveland's Message 34
      President Clinton Signs the "Apology Resolution" 34
   The Appropriate Remedy for Treason 38
      A Word Study of "Restitution" 38

Professor Francis A. Boyle Discusses the Remedy 39

The Proper Remedy is Provided by the King of Hawai'i 40

Part 3 Introducing the King of Hawai'i 42

Ali'i Nui Mō'i Edmund Keli'i Silva, Jr. 42

The Royal Genealogy of King Edmund Keli'i Silva, Jr. 43

Growing Recognition of King Edmund Keli'i Silva, Jr. 50

Lamaku Mikahala Roy 50

Pearl Means 51

98 Year Old Kupuna, Auntie Ku'uipo (Ipo) Kanehele 52

Moving the Kingdom Forward 53

King Keli'i Offers an Invitation to Unite as One People 53

Seeking the Path of Aloha 56

A Different Sort of King 56

A Study of Plato's Philosopher Kings 60

Plato Teaches - a Philosopher Should Be the Navigator 61

Plato's Philosopher King 62

A Poem for King Edmund Keli'i Silva, Jr. 64

Part 4 The Kingdom is Restored by King Edmund Keli'i Silva, Jr. .. 65

Kingdom Restoration 65

The Montevideo Convention Supports Restoration 65

The King Discusses the Illegal Overthrow 66

The United States Offers No Justice or Remedy 67

King Keli'i Creates a Plan to Restore Hawai'i 69

The Constitutional Monarchy Explained 70

The Flag of the Kingdom of Hawai'i 73

Hō'ili'ili Nani - the Gathering of Beautiful Things 74

Part 5 Hālau Aomaluhiamauloa 80

Promoting Peace Throughout the World 80

A Letter to Secretary-General Ban Ki-moon 82

Part 6 Queen Lili'uokalani's Last Words 90
   Pictures of the Annexation Ceremony 90
   Queen Lili'uokalani's Reminder "God is Not Mocked" 91
      Hawaii's Story by Queen Lili'uokalani 91
Part 7 Current Issues 94
   The Aloha Aina Project 94
      Executive Summary of the Aloha Aina Project 94
      Ali'i Mana'o Nui Lanny Sinkin on the Aloha Aina Project 98
   Nation within a Nation 99
      The False Narrative: Hiding the Truth 99
      King Keli'i Silva Jr. Discusses "Nation within a Nation" 101
      The Kingdom is Purposely Excluded 103
      Pearl Means Warns the Hawaiian People 104
      King Keli'i Summarizes "Nation within a Nation" 105
      Aunty Ipo Addresses State-Controlled Division 107
   Mauna a Wākea 108
      The Mauna a Wākea Protectors 108
      The Sacred Mountain of Akua 109
      Protecting the Protectors 111
      Mauna a Wākea Receives National Attention 112
      Kingdom Litigation 114
   Until the Kingdom of Hawai'i is Totally Independent 115
      Reaffirmation of Independence 115
Part 8 Resolved Issues 124
   The King's Imprisonment and the Royal Kupuna Exchange 124
      Facts According to Ali'i Mana'o Nui Lanny Sinkin 124
Part 9 The Man, as King 130
   Truth Comes in Two Faces 130
Epilogue 142

We Continue on a Righteous Path 142
    It is Time! 142
    Freedom is a Gift 153
References 154
About the Author 163
    Coming Soon... A Sequel to "The Invisible King" 164

Book Cover Pictures

1. Governor Sanford B. Dole, Territory of Hawaii
2. 1897 Ku'e Anti-Annexation Petition (7500 Men & 11,000 Women)
3. Queen's Protest Against Annexation (in the Hawaiian language)
4. The Provisional Government Cabinet -
   James A. King, Sanford B. Dole, W.O. Smith, P.C. Jones
5. Lili'uokalani ~ Queen of Hawai'i
6. Minister John L. Stevens
7. Republic of Hawai'i Government
8. The USS Boston's landing force at the Arlington Hotel, in Honolulu on 1/16/1893
9. Lili'uokalani - the Illegally Overthrown Queen
10. Present Day King – Edmund Keli'i Silva, Jr.

Po'o Huna 'Ano, Kumaka.
'O ke Ali'i Nui Mo'i a 'Ō Ke Aupuni ō Hawai'i.
Ku I Ka Mana Hawai'i Nei.

The Invisible King

"I am Edmund Keli'i Silva, Jr., direct lineal descendent of King Kamehameha 'Ai Lu'au, and under authority of the Hawaiian Constitution in effect on January 17, 1893, I hereby declare Hawai'i to be an independent, Sovereign Nation. In the name of Almighty God and of my people, I hereby declare the Nation of Hawai'i to be free and Independent from the influence and authority of any and all other nations. In the name of Almighty God and of my people, I hereby declare the Nation of Hawai'i to be a Sovereign Kingdom grounded in the noble culture of an old and honorable people. Na ke Kauoha o ke Akua Manamana Loa." [3]

King Edmund Keli'i Silva, Jr.
June 23, 2003

Ku I Ka Mana
The Mana of All Hawai'i is Rising

Preface

Originally, I was going to title the book, *"Ku I Ka Mana Hawai'i Nei"*, which means, *"The Mana of All Hawai'i is Rising"*. Even though I changed the title, I kept the original background picture on the book cover, which symbolizes this very thought.

"Ku I Ka Mana" is the title of the Kingdom's Chant.[1] The chant describes exactly what is happening in Hawai'i now – that is, the Kingdom of Hawai'i is being restored, and returned to its pre-1893 government, by King Edmund Keli'i Silva, Jr.

Instead of using *Ku I Ka Mana Hawai'i Nei* as the title, I decided on, *The Invisible King*, which comes from a letter I wrote in 2014.[2] **I believe Edmund Keli'i Silva, Jr. will emerge from behind the mist, to bring peace and harmony to our planet as King of the Hawaiian Nation.** My favorite passage from the letter is below, and expresses why I call King Keli'i - "The Invisible King".

> *I believe that King Keli'i is "of the light" --- a Light Warrior --- here on this planet to do a tremendous work. Light itself cannot be seen; rather, it is experienced.*
>
> *Also, I believe King Keli'i's humble nature contributes to his being an INVISIBLE KING. King Keli'i is not out in the streets shouting, "I am King, look at me". Instead, he has clothed himself with humility and dignity ---- his light and love hidden within him, and radiating out.*

It is a known fact that most historical books are less than exciting to read; but please, do not discount the miraculous fact of KU I KA MANA HAWAI'I NEI. This is a story worth exploring and spending a little time with.

HEAR THE VOICES OF THE ANCESTORS, WHOSE MANA IS AMONG US. THEIR VOICES ARE CALLING FOR THE KINGDOM OF HAWAI'I AT THIS VERY MOMENT IN HISTORY. THE ANCESTORS ARE CALLING OUT TO US, THE PEOPLE OF THE LIGHT, AND CALLING TO THE LANDS OF HAWAI'I NEI – TO RISE UP, TO BE COURAGEOUS, AND TO HELP OUR KING RESTORE AND RETURN THE KINGDOM OF HAWAI'I TO HER RIGHTFUL PLACE AMONG THE NATIONS.

IT IS TIME!

Introduction

I recognize that there are strong emotions and opinions attached to the subject of Kingdom restoration - over a century's worth of differing views. So in this book, I'll present the facts, and hope I inspire you to join those of us who believe in, and are working towards, full restoration of the Kingdom of Hawai'i.

If you're like most people I've talked to, your ideal vacation spot would be in the beautiful islands of Hawaii. Hawaii's romantic reputation has woven its way into our collective consciousness as "paradise on earth". I agree, Hawaii truly was a paradise on earth (for over a thousand years), but I don't believe this is true any longer. The very heart of the Hawaiian Islands was viciously ripped out, and replaced with an empty, manufactured "artificial heart" – leaving the islands in an unnatural, vulnerable condition. In fact; it has been said by the King, "We are a nation that was stolen, and left with decapitated spirits." [3]

IN THIS BOOK, I'LL EXPOSE WHAT REALLY HAPPENED IN 1893 TO THIS ISLAND PARADISE AT THE HANDS OF THE UNITED STATES. I'VE SUMMARIZED THESE TREASONOUS EVENTS IN THE BOOK TITLE - CONSPIRACY, INVASION, OVERTHROW AND ILLEGAL OCCUPATION. BUT IT GOES EVEN FURTHER THAN THAT WITH THE STATEMENT, "THE SEIZURE OF THE KINGDOM WAS AN ILLEGAL ACT OF WAR." [4]

By exposing these tragic events, I hope to inspire people to wake up to the truth, and prevent the complete extinction of the Hawaiian culture.

In Hawaii's past, there was something unique and magical that no other nation has ever been able to duplicate. It is Hawaii's "Aloha Spirit", which permeated everything and everyone. Sadly though, the *Aloha Spirit* seems to have become more of a "product", manufactured to sell tourism in Hawaii. The true *Aloha Spirit* exists behind the scenes – far from where tourists show up. Much of it is found in the last remnants of Hawaiian culture, as well as among those who work towards Hawaiian Sovereignty.

I wrote this book for two reasons. The first reason is to introduce you to the true history of the Hawaiian Islands and expose exactly what happened in 1893 that led to the "decapitation" of the Hawaiian Spirit, and ultimately led to the Hawaiian nation becoming the 50th state of the United States of America in 1959.

The second reason I wrote this book is to introduce you to a very important person – King Edmund Keli'i Silva, Jr., and present you with what he is doing to return the Kingdom of Hawai'i to nation status, and restore the nation to the form of government that it once was – a Constitutional Monarchy.

QUEEN LILI'UOKALANI DIED IN 1917 BELIEVING UNTIL HER VERY LAST BREATH THAT HER NATION WOULD BE RESTORED. IN 2003, THE KINGDOM OF HAWAI'I WAS LEGALLY RESTORED BY THE QUEEN'S COUSIN, KING EDMUND KELI'I SILVA, JR.

If you're like most people, you probably didn't realize that such tragic events took place in Hawaii. You probably also didn't know that there is a Sovereignty movement in Hawaii, much less that there exists a legitimate King of Hawai'i.

For those of you who can't imagine a real King of Hawai'i, I can assure you that he has been given a mandate to BE King. **King Edmund Keli'i Silva, Jr. was selected by the House of Nobles, as High Chief / King (Ali'i Nui Mō'i), in 2002.**

I hope that after you read this book, you'll be inspired to support King Keli'i in his mighty work – the work of exposing the true story about Hawai'i's past, and the work of fully restoring the Kingdom of Hawai'i to nation status. This he has been doing for a lifetime, and especially since 2002. He has dedicated himself to Kingdom Restoration - day by day, letter by letter, and speech by speech.

It is my view that King Edmund Keli'i Silva, Jr. has been ignored by those who would greatly benefit by him – people in Hawai'i and people all over this planet; yet it is not because people aren't interested in Hawaiian Sovereignty or in what he is doing, but because the truth has been so cleverly hidden and covered up for over 120 years.

FOR MANY PEOPLE, IT HAS BEEN ALMOST IMPOSSIBLE TO GRASP THE MANDATE THAT WAS GIVEN TO KING KELI'I (BY THE HOUSE OF NOBLES) TO ACTUALLY BE KING – AT THIS TIME, AND AT THIS VERY MOMENT IN HISTORY.

Even though there have been a multitude of challenges, King Keli'i is making an impact on behalf of the Kingdom. His words have great power, and are going out and into the universe, making a significant difference.

For those of us who understand his mission, we are experiencing the magnificent awakening of people all over the world, as they learn the truth about Hawai'i's past and what Hawai'i means to our planet's future. People have begun to recognize the treachery that befell the Queen of Hawai'i and her nation, and they no longer wish to see the United States continue their illegal occupation of the Hawaiian Islands.

How I arrived with such a desire to see the Kingdom of Hawai'i restored is this: since 1983, I have been a natural health and wellness advocate, having written many books on these subjects over the last several years.

A few years ago, I turned my attention to the health and wellness of our planet. Having lived in Hawaii for over ten years, I understood her true history, and knew that our beloved planet needs exactly what the Kingdom of Hawai'i will provide to the planet, once restored. Our planet needs passionate people that understand Mother Earth's needs, and wish to see her return to vibrant health. During the restoration process, **the Kingdom of Hawai'i will begin to implement the *Aloha Aina Project*,** [5, 18] **which will be seen as an important catalyst for the sustainability / cleansing / detoxification of not only Hawai'i, but our entire planet**.

The *Aloha Aina Project* is an amazing blueprint that was commissioned by King Keli'i – not only for restoring health and vitality to the people, the land and the culture of Hawai'i; but also, as a blueprint for all the nations to reach their fullest potential. You can find out more about the *Aloha Aina Project* in Part 7.

THE ALOHA AINA PROJECT IS THE KEY TO PREVENTING TOTAL EXTINCTION OF THE HAWAIIAN CULTURE, AND IS THE SOLUTION TO THE VUNERABILITY OF THE HAWAIIAN PEOPLE TO THE EXPLOITATION OF IMPORTED GOODS INSTIGATED BY THE UNITED STATES GOVERNMENT AND ITS PROXY, THE HAWAIIAN STATE GOVERNMENT.

In addition to the *Aloha Aina Project,* **I am also very excited about the Peace Center which King Keli'i has envisioned for the Hawaiian Kingdom.** The King has shared that the Peace Center will be a place where "nations will stand in solidarity as one voice and one people to protect the earth, land to sea, from unprecedented destruction..." The Peace Center is called, *Hālau Aomaluhiamauloa,* which means the House of Enlightenment and Peace. You can find out more about the Peace Center in Part 5.

Now, I would like to share an inspirational quote from Ali'i Mana'o Nui Lanny Sinkin, [65] Chief Advisor to King Keli'i, as he provides us with the Kingdom's *raison d'etre,* and a summary of what I feel will be the future role of the Kingdom of Hawai'i throughout the world.

> *The overall theme of the Kingdom work is peace and reconciliation within the Human Family, and peace and reconciliation between the Human Family and the rest of the Natural World.*
>
> *The mana of all Hawai'i is rising. There is a wide spread awakening to both the truth of what happened in the past, and the answer to be found in the restored Kingdom. That awakening is taking place in many areas and many people of courage are stepping forward to contribute to the awakening.*

Love and Light...
Alie James

Part 1
Proof of Queen Lili'uokalani's Illegal Overthrow in 1893

THE OVERTHROW OF THE KINGDOM OF HAWAI'I FACTS ACCORDING TO QUEEN LILI'UOKALANI

In 1893, On the Beautiful Island of Oahu...

Let us begin with Queen Lili'uokalani's own words,[15] as it was she whose Nation was viciously and illegally overthrown on January 17, 1893.

I Liliuokalani, by the Grace of God and under the Constitution of the Hawaiian Kingdom, Queen, do hereby solemnly protest against any and all acts done against myself and the Constitutional Government of the Hawaiian Kingdom by certain persons claiming to have established a Provisional Government of and for this Kingdom.

That I yield to the superior force of the United States of America whose Minister Plenipotentiary, His Excellency John L. Stevens, has caused United States troops to be landed at Honolulu and declared that he would support the Provisional Government.

Now to avoid any collision of armed forces, and perhaps the loss of life, I do this under protest and impelled by said force yield my authority until such time as the Government of the United States shall, upon facts being presented to it, undo the action of its representatives and reinstate me in the authority which I claim as the Constitutional Sovereign of the Hawaiian Islands.

Done at Honolulu this 17th day of January, A.D. 1893.

ADMISSION OF GUILT - PUBLIC LAW 103-150

Following the Queen's words, we now have the "whereas" statements, which I have excerpted from Public Law 103-150.[5, 18] This law was passed by the 103rd Congress of the United States in 1993. Public Law 103-150 is now known as the *"Apology Resolution"*, and was signed by President Bill Clinton on the 100th anniversary of the illegal overthrow of the Hawaiian Kingdom.

"Whereas" Statements are the Preamble to Legislation

Please keep in mind, that when the word, "whereas", is placed at the beginning of a legislative bill (in its preamble) it means, "because". Following the word, "whereas" are statements of fact that justify the enactment of the legislation. [6]

Therefore, we know that the "whereas" statements in the Apology Resolution are agreed upon statements of fact, and these facts are the reason for enacting the legislation. It is also important to note, that many of these facts were derived from President Grover Cleveland's message to the Senate and House on December 18, 1893, as you will see in Part 2.

"Whereas" Statements of Public Law 103-150

Below, are the "whereas" statements found in the *Apology Resolution*,[5] and these provide you with legislative proof that the Kingdom of Hawai'i was recognized as a Sovereign Nation, held international treaties, and that it was subjected to Conspiracy, Invasion, Overthrow and Illegal Occupation by the United States:

> *Whereas,*
> *prior to the arrival of the first Europeans in 1778, the Native Hawaiian people lived in a highly organized, self-sufficient, subsistent social system based on communal land tenure with a sophisticated language, culture, and religion;*
>
> *Whereas,*
> *a unified monarchical government of the Hawaiian Islands was established in 1810 under Kamehameha I, the first King of Hawaii;*
>
> *Whereas,*
> *from 1826 until 1893, the United States recognized the independence of the Kingdom of Hawaii, extended full and complete diplomatic recognition to the Hawaiian Government, and entered into treaties and conventions with the Hawaiian monarchs to govern commerce and navigation in 1826, 1842, 1849, 1875, and 1887;*

Whereas,
the Congregational Church (now known as the United Church of Christ), through its American Board of Commissioners for Foreign Missions, sponsored and sent more than 100 missionaries to the Kingdom of Hawaii between 1820 and 1850;

Whereas,
on January 14, 1893, John L. Stevens (hereafter referred to in this Resolution as the "United States Minister"), the United States Minister assigned to the sovereign and independent Kingdom of Hawaii conspired with a small group of non-Hawaiian residents of the Kingdom of Hawaii, including citizens of the United States, to overthrow the indigenous and lawful Government of Hawaii;

Whereas,
in pursuance of the conspiracy to overthrow the Government of Hawaii, the United States Minister and the naval representatives of the United States caused armed naval forces of the United States to invade the sovereign Hawaiian nation on January 16, 1893, and to position themselves near the Hawaiian Government buildings and the Iolani Palace to intimidate Queen Liliuokalani and her Government;

Whereas,
on the afternoon of January 17, 1893, a Committee of Safety that represented the American and European sugar planters, descendants of missionaries and financiers deposed the Hawaiian monarchy and proclaimed the establishment of a Provisional Government;

Whereas,
the United States Minister thereupon extended diplomatic recognition to the Provisional Government that was formed by the conspirators without the consent of the Native Hawaiian people or the lawful Government of Hawaii and in violation of treaties between the two nations and of international law;

Whereas,
soon thereafter, when informed of the risk of bloodshed with resistance, Queen Liliuokalani issued the following statement yielding her authority to the United States Government rather than to the Provisional Government:

"I, Liliuokalani, by the Grace of God and under the Constitution of the Hawaiian Kingdom, Queen, do hereby solemnly protest against any and all acts one against myself and the Constitutional Government of the Hawaiian Kingdom by certain persons claiming to have established a Provisional Government of and for this Kingdom.

That I yield to the superior force of the United States of America whose Minister Plenipotentiary, His Excellency John L. Stevens, has caused United States troops to be landed a Honolulu and declared that he would support the Provisional Government.

Now to avoid any collision of armed forces, and perhaps the loss of life, I do this under protest and impelled by said force yield my authority until such time as the Government of the United States shall, upon facts being presented to it, undo the action of its representatives and reinstate me in the authority which I claim as the Constitutional Sovereign of the Hawaiian Islands.

Done at Honolulu this 17th day of January, A.D. 1893."

'Iolani Palace, 1893

Whereas,

without the active support and intervention by the United States diplomatic and military representatives, the insurrection against the Government of Queen Liliuokalani would have failed for lack of popular support and insufficient arms;

Whereas,

on February 1, 1893, the United States Minister raised the American flag and proclaimed Hawaii to be a protectorate of the United States;

Whereas,

the report of a Presidentially established investigation conducted by former Congressman James Blount [7] *into the events surrounding the insurrection and overthrow of January 17, 1893, concluded that the United States diplomatic and military representatives had abused their authority and were responsible for the change in government;*

Whereas,

as a result of this investigation, the United States Minister to Hawaii was recalled from his diplomatic post and the military commander of the United States armed forces stationed in Hawaii was disciplined and forced to resign his commission;

Whereas,

in a message to Congress on December 18, 1893, President Grover Cleveland reported fully and accurately on the illegal acts of the conspirators, described such acts as an "act of war, committed with the participation of a diplomatic representative of the United States and without authority of Congress", and acknowledged that by such acts the government of a peaceful and friendly people was overthrown;

*Whereas,
President Cleveland further concluded that a "substantial wrong has thus been done which a due regard for our national character as well as the rights of the injured people requires we should endeavor to repair" and called for the restoration of the Hawaiian monarchy;*

*Whereas,
the Provisional Government protested President Cleveland's call for the restoration of the monarchy and continued to hold state power and pursue annexation to the United States;*

*Whereas,
the Provisional Government successfully lobbied the Committee on Foreign Relations of the Senate (hereafter referred to in this Resolution as the "Committee") to conduct a new investigation into the events surrounding the overthrow of the monarchy;*

*Whereas,
the Committee and its chairman, Senator John Morgan, conducted hearings in Washington, D.C., from December 27, 1893, through February 26, 1894, in which members of the Provisional Government justified and condoned the actions of the United States Minister and recommended annexation of Hawaii;*

Whereas,
although the Provisional Government was able to obscure the role of the United States in the illegal overthrow of the Hawaiian monarchy, it was unable to rally the support from two-thirds of the Senate needed to ratify a treaty of annexation;

Whereas,
on July 4, 1894, the Provisional Government declared itself to be the Republic of Hawaii;

Whereas,
on January 24, 1895, while imprisoned in Iolani Palace, Queen Liliuokalani was forced by representatives of the Republic of Hawaii to officially abdicate her throne;

Whereas,
in the 1896 United States Presidential election, William McKinley replaced Grover Cleveland;

Whereas,
on July 7, 1898, as a consequence of the Spanish-American War, President McKinley signed the Newlands Joint Resolution [8] *that provided for the annexation of Hawaii;*

Whereas,
through the Newlands Resolution, the self-declared Republic of Hawaii ceded sovereignty over the Hawaiian Islands to the United States;

Whereas,
the Republic of Hawaii also ceded 1,800,000 acres [7,280 km²] of crown, government and public lands of the Kingdom of Hawaii, without the consent of or compensation to the Native Hawaiian people of Hawaii or their sovereign government;

Whereas,
the Congress, through the Newlands Resolution, ratified the cession, annexed Hawaii as part of the United States, and vested title to the lands in Hawaii in the United States;

Whereas,
the Newlands Resolution also specified that treaties existing between Hawaii and foreign nations were to immediately cease and be replaced by United States treaties with such nations;

Whereas,
the Newlands Resolution effected the transaction between the Republic of Hawaii and the United States Government;

Whereas,
the indigenous Hawaiian people never directly relinquished their claims to their inherent sovereignty as a people or over their national lands to the United States, either through their monarchy or through a plebiscite or referendum;

Whereas,
on April 30, 1900, President McKinley signed the Organic Act [9] that provided a government for the territory of Hawaii and defined the political structure and powers of the newly established Territorial Government and its relationship to the United States;

Whereas,
on August 21, 1959, Hawaii became the 50th State of the United States;

Whereas,
the health and well-being of the Native Hawaiian people is intrinsically tied to their deep feelings and attachment to the land;

Whereas,
the long-range economic and social changes in Hawaii over the nineteenth and early twentieth centuries have been devastating to the population and to the health and well-being of the Hawaiian people;

Whereas,
the Native Hawaiian people are determined to preserve, develop and transmit to future generations their ancestral territory, and their cultural identity in accordance with their own spiritual and traditional beliefs, customs, practices, language, and social institutions;

Whereas,
in order to promote racial harmony and cultural understanding, the Legislature of the State of Hawaii has determined that the year 1993, should serve Hawaii as a year of special reflection on the rights

and dignities of the Native Hawaiians in the Hawaiian and the American societies;

Whereas,
the Eighteenth General Synod of the United Church of Christ in recognition of the denomination's historical complicity in the illegal overthrow of the Kingdom of Hawaii in 1893 directed the Office of the President of the United Church of Christ to offer a public apology to the Native Hawaiian people and to initiate the process of reconciliation between the United Church of Christ and the Native Hawaiians; and

Whereas,
it is proper and timely for the Congress on the occasion of the impending one hundredth anniversary of the event, to acknowledge the historic significance of the illegal overthrow of the Kingdom of Hawaii, to express its deep regret to the Native Hawaiian people, and to support the reconciliation efforts of the State of Hawaii and the United Church of Christ with Native Hawaiians;

Now, therefore, be it resolved by the Senate and House of Representatives of the United States of America in Congress assembled...

What follows the "whereas" statements is an acknowledgement of these facts, and an official apology; however, it is no surprise that the people of Hawai'i are still waiting on the restitution that is due to them for such horrendous, treasonous acts committed against their innocent nation.

Now that we have established the facts and circumstances that led to the overthrow of the Hawaiian nation, we are left with the question of WHY. Although the answer can only be known by the treasonous Conspirators, I will offer my opinion as to WHY THEY DID WHAT THEY DID, based on my research:

THE UNITED STATES MINISTER (JOHN L. STEVENS), THE MEMBERS AND SUPPORTERS OF THE SAFETY COMMITTEE, AND SUBSEQUENTLY THE SELF-APPOINTED PROVISIONAL GOVERNMENT, WERE MEN AND WOMEN WITHOUT CHARACTER, WHO HAD NO HEART, AND NO HONOR OR RESPECT TOWARD THEIR HOST NATION. THEY COVETED A PROSPEROUS NATION THAT WAS NOT THEIRS. THEY WERE FILLED WITH GREED AND LUST FOR POWER.

In fact, these men and women have the great distinction of finishing what began in 1778 with Captain Cook --- they totally and completely ripped the heart and soul out of Hawai'i Nei. A whole nation was decimated, desecrated and ultimately, decapitated because of their filthy lust and covetousness for the Kingdom of Hawai'i.

To further enhance my viewpoint about the arrogance of the men and women involved in the conspiracy to overthrow the Queen, here is an excerpt from President Cleveland's letter to Congress in December of 1893 [12] in regards to the US Minister John L. Stevens [bold text added]:

> *On the 19th day of November, 1892, nearly two months before the first overt act tending towards the subversion of the Hawaiian Government and the attempted transfer of Hawaiian territory to the United States, he [Minister Stevens] addressed a long letter to the Secretary of State in which the case for*

annexation was elaborately argued, on moral, political, and economical grounds. He refers to the loss of the Hawaiian sugar interests from the operation of the McKinley bill, and the tendency to still further depreciation of sugar property unless some positive measure of relief is granted.

He [Minister Stevens] strongly inveighs against the existing Hawaiian Government and emphatically declares for annexation. ***He says: "In truth the monarchy here is an absurd anachronism. It has nothing on which it logically or legitimately stands. The feudal basis on which it once stood no longer existing, the monarchy now is only an impediment to good government - an obstruction to the prosperity and progress of the islands."***

In contrast to the evil intent of these rogue United States Conspirators, and as they were implementing their plans of annexation over the course of several years, Queen Lili'uokalani held on to her Christian foundation and belief that the United States would do the right thing and restore her as Queen, and the Hawaiian Kingdom to the Hawaiian people. In 1897, she took a trip to Washington, DC, and while there, wrote that she was "quietly awaiting the course of justice and conscious of the strength derived from truth and right on my side".

THE TREATY OF ANNEXATION

Queen Lili'uokalani Protests Against the Treaty of Annexation

Unfortunately, no justice was forthcoming; in fact, quite the opposite - a proposed treaty to cede the Islands of Hawaii to the territory and dominion of the United States was signed in Washington D.C. by Francis March Hatch, Lorrin A. Thurston, and William A. Kinney. In protest, the Queen sent her secretaries, Mr. Joseph Heleluhe and Captain Julius A. Palmer, to the Department of State with the following protest: [10]

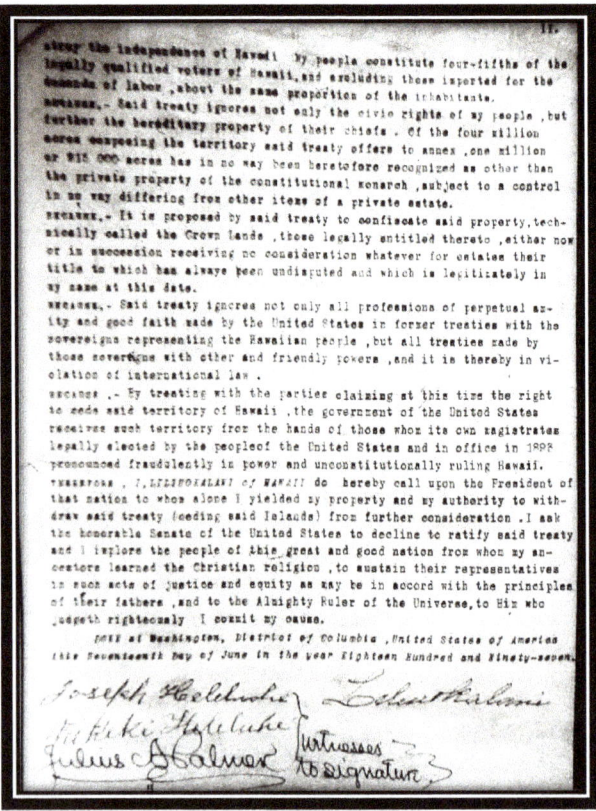

MY OFFICIAL PROTEST TO THE TREATY

I, LILIUOKALANI of Hawaii, by the will of God named heir apparent on the tenth day of April, A. D. 1877, and by the grace of God Queen of the Hawaiian Islands on the seventeenth day of January, A. D. 1893, do hereby protest against the ratification of a certain treaty, which, so I am informed, has been signed at Washington by Messrs. Hatch, Thurston, and Kinney, purporting to cede those Islands to the territory and dominion of the United States. I declare such a treaty to be an act of wrong toward the native and part-native people of Hawaii, an invasion of the rights of the ruling chiefs, in violation of international rights both toward my people and toward friendly nations with whom they have made treaties, the perpetuation of the fraud whereby the constitutional government was overthrown and, finally, an act of gross injustice to me.

Because the official protests made by me on the seventeenth day of January, 1893, to the so-called Provisional Government was signed by me, and received by said government with the assurance that the case was referred to the United States of America for arbitration.

YIELDED TO AVOID BLOODSHED.

Because that protest and my communications to the United States Government immediately thereafter expressly declare that I yielded my authority to the forces of the United States in order to avoid bloodshed, and because I recognized the futility of a conflict with so formidable a power.

Because the President of the United States, the Secretary of State, and an envoy commissioned by them reported in official documents that my government was unlawfully coerced by the forces, diplomatic and naval, of the United States; that I was at the date of their investigations the constitutional ruler of my people.

Because such decision of the recognized magistrates of the United States was officially communicated to me and to Sanford B. Dole, and said Dole's resignation requested by Albert S. Willis, the recognized agent and minister of the Government of the United States.

Because neither the above-named commission nor the government which sends it has ever received any such authority from the registered voters of Hawaii, but derives its assumed powers from the so-called committee of public safety, organized on or about the seventeenth day of January, 1893, said committee being composed largely of persons claiming American citizenship, and not one single Hawaiian was a member thereof, or in any way participated in the demonstration leading to its existence.

Because my people, about forty thousand in number, have in no way been consulted by those, three thousand in number, who claim the right to destroy the independence of Hawaii. My people constitute four-fifths of the legally qualified voters of Hawaii, and excluding those imported for the demands of labor, about the same proportion of the inhabitants.

CIVIC AND HEREDITARY RIGHTS.

Because said treaty ignores, not only the civic rights of my people, but, further, the hereditary property of their chiefs. Of the 4,000,000 acres composing the territory said treaty offers to annex, 1,000,000 or 915,000 acres has in no way been heretofore recognized as other than the private property of the constitutional monarch, subject to a control in no way differing from other items of a private estate.

Because it is proposed by said treaty to confiscate said property, technically called the crown lands, those legally entitled thereto, either now or in succession, receiving no consideration whatever for estates, their title to which has been always undisputed, and which is legitimately in my name at this date.

Because said treaty ignores, not only all professions of perpetual amity and good faith made by the United States in former treaties with the sovereigns representing the Hawaiian people, but all treaties made by those sovereigns with other and friendly powers, and it is thereby in violation of international law.

Because, by treating with the parties claiming at this time the right to cede said territory of Hawaii, the Government of the United States receives such territory from the hands of those whom its own magistrates (legally elected by the people of the United States, and in office in 1893) pronounced fraudulently in power and unconstitutionally ruling Hawaii.

APPEALS TO PRESIDENT AND SENATE.

Therefore I, Liliuokalani of Hawaii, do hereby call upon the President of that nation, to whom alone I yielded my property and my authority, to withdraw said treaty (ceding said Islands) from further consideration. I ask the honorable Senate of the United States to decline to ratify said treaty, and I implore the people of this great and good nation, from whom my ancestors learned the Christian religion, to sustain their representatives in such acts of justice and equity as may be in accord with the principles of their fathers, and to the Almighty Ruler of the universe, to him who judgeth righteously, I commit my cause.

Done at Washington, District of Columbia, United States of America, this seventeenth day of June, in the year eighteen hundred and ninety-seven.

"LILIUOKALANI.

"JOSEPH HELELUH.

"WOKEKI HELELUHE.   Witnesses to Signature

"JULIUS A. PALMER.

The Hawaiian People Protest Against Annexation by Signing the Ku'e Petition

Not only did the Queen protest against annexation to the United States, but so did the Hawaiian people. The two Ku'e Petitions (men and women) were signed by 38,000 out of 40,000 Kanaka Maoli, which means that 95% of the Hawaiian people protested against annexation.[11]

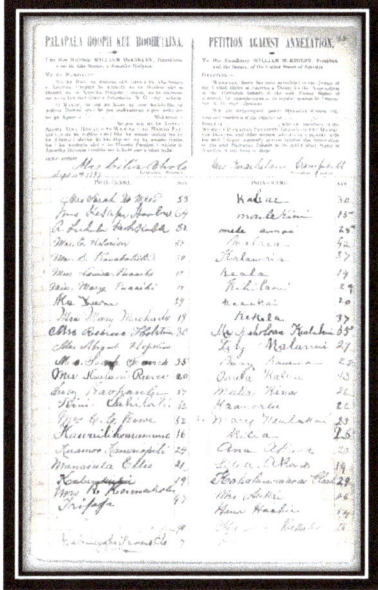

Signatures of the Women

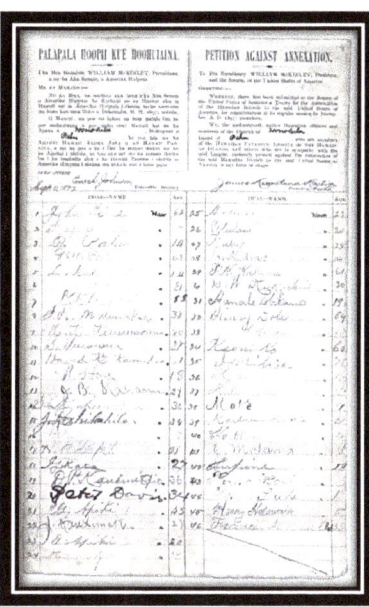

Signatures of the Men

*Despite the Protest of the Queen
& the Hawaiian People,
the "False Flag" of the United States
is Raised in 1898*

THE UNDENIABLE, INDISPUTABLE TRUTH... CONSPIRACY, INVASION, OVERTHROW & ILLEGAL OCCUPATION OF THE KINGDOM OF HAWAI'I

The Kingdom of Hawai'i Is Due Full Restoration and Restitution

Although there is much more to this tragic story, you now have linkage between Queen Lili'uokalani's documented protests, and Public Law 103-150. You can now see DEFINITIVE PROOF that the United States conspired, invaded, overthrew and illegally occupied the Hawaiian Kingdom, which was a friendly nation.

BECAUSE OF THIS NOW KNOWN FACT OF HISTORY, THE KINGDOM OF HAWAI'I IS DUE FULL RESTORATION AND RESTITUTION BY THE PERPETRATORS OF THIS EVENT – THE UNITED STATES GOVERNMENT.

We are now more than 120 years past this shameful event, and the people of Hawai'i are still waiting for the United States to fully restore the Kingdom of Hawai'i to the sovereign nation that it once was.

Sadly, we realize that what was true then, is still true today --- that there was, and is an oligarchy that manipulates the media, congress and governmental officials to create the exact outcome they so desire – this is true in the state of Hawaii, the United States, and all over the world. It is imperative that we work to create the outcome we so desire (as believers of truth, freedom and justice). The outcome that we want is the full restoration of the Hawaiian Nation.

I believe we now have an advantage. The truth of this event is no longer able to be hidden, and it is slowly being revealed. One day soon, the illegal occupation of Hawai'i by the United States government will come to an end, and in its place, the restored Kingdom of Hawai'i will be revealed to the whole world, along with her King, Edmund Keli'i Silva, Jr.

Part 2
Story Details

FORGIVENESS AND THE ALOHA SPIRIT

Should the Nations of the World Be Forgiven?

Should the nations of the world be forgiven for their ignorance and lack of support for the Hawaiian people over the last 120 years?

Perhaps the lies, deceit and revised history that have been told and written by the "state controlled" American media and printing presses over the last 12 decades have resulted in a naïve, world-wide belief that the Kingdom of Hawai'i was simply "honored" to be swallowed up and into the 50th state of the United States.

DOES IGNORANCE AND NAIVETY JUSTIFY FORGIVENESS?

HAVING THE SPIRIT OF ALOHA WITHIN ONE'S HEART WOULD SUGGEST, YES! I BELIEVE FORGIVENESS IS AN APPROPRIATE RESPONSE FOR THE LACK OF SUPPORT TO THE HAWAIIAN PEOPLE. I BASE THIS ON MY SINCERE BELIEF THAT THE SPIRIT OF ALOHA IS THE HEARTBEAT OF THE KINGDOM OF HAWAI'I.

Going Forward, Ignorance is Not Acceptable

As stated, I believe that forgiveness is an appropriate response for the lack of support of the Hawaiian people in the past, but I also believe that now, ignorance of Hawai'i's history is no longer an acceptable excuse. This is because the truth is easily documented and available for verification.

The illegal invasion of the Kingdom of Hawai'i by the uninvited military force of the United States on January 17, 1893, and the continued illegal occupation of the Kingdom of Hawai'i by the United States government and their subordinate government - the Hawaiian State government, is well documented – even by two former Presidents (Cleveland & Clinton) of the United States.

Troops in Front of 'Iolani Palace during the Overthrow of Queen Lili'uokalani

TWO AMERICAN PRESIDENTS AGREE...
THE UNITED STATES ILLEGALLY INVADED & OVERTHREW THE KINGDOM OF HAWAI'I AND HER QUEEN, LILI'UOKALANI

President Grover Cleveland

One need only look at the facts of the overthrow presented by President Grover Cleveland (the President of the United States at the time of Hawai'i's overthrow), to be completely convinced of this horrible truth.

President Cleveland delivered a message to Congress in December 1893. His message was filled with a multitude of facts about the U.S. invasion of the friendly nation of Hawai'i and her Queen, by the ruse (conspiracy) of American businessmen.

BECAUSE OF PRESIDENT CLEVELAND'S MORAL STANCE, AND KNOWLEDGE OF THE ILLEGALITY OF THE U.S. OVERTHROW, HE REFUSED TO SUPPORT THE TREATY OF ANNEXATION --- HE DID THIS BY REFUSING TO SEND THE TREATY TO THE SENATE FOR CONSIDERATION.

Sadly though, President Cleveland's successor, President William McKinley, did not possess the same morals, and was an opportunist, so he allowed annexation to take place in 1898 via the *Newlands Joint Resolution*.[8]

President Bill Clinton

It is important to note, that 100 years later, in 1993, President Clinton signed the *Apology Resolution*,[5] which drew many of its "whereas" facts from President Cleveland's 1893 archived message to Congress.[2]

JUST LIKE PRESIDENT CLEVELAND BEFORE HIM, PRESIDENT CLINTON ADMITED (BY HIS SIGNING OF THE APOLOGY RESOLUTION), TO THE ILLEGAL INVASION OF HONOLULU (WHICH WAS THE SEAT OF THE CONSTITUTIONAL MONARCHY OF THE HAWAIIAN KINGDOM) BY THE UNITED STATES.

Unfortunately, the *Apology Resolution* did not go far enough because it did not provide the remedy of restitution. Instead it "supports reconciliation", and reconciliation is NOT the proper remedy under international law.

The only acceptable remedy is restitution when there is such blatant, treasonous violation of treaties - at the time of the invasion, the Treaties of Friendship, Commerce & Navigation existed between the U.S and the Hawaiian Kingdom.[13] And not only was there the violation of those three treaties, there was an armed invasion by the United States of a friendly nation.

President Grover Cleveland's Message to the Senate & House on December 18, 1893

Below are excerpts of President Cleveland's speech:[12]

I believe that a candid and thorough examination of the facts will force the conviction that 'the provisional government owes its existence to an armed invasion by the United States...

The lawful Government of Hawaii was overthrown without the drawing of a sword or the firing of a shot...

A brief statement of the occurrences that led to the subversion of the constitutional Government of Hawaii in the interests of annexation to the United States...

She [Queen Lili'uokalani] surrendered not to the provisional government, but the United States. She surrendered not absolutely and permanently, but temporarily and conditionally until such time as the facts could be considered by the United States... not merely to avoid bloodshed, but because she could place implicit reliance upon the justice of the United States...

President Clinton Signs the "Apology Resolution"- Public Law 103-150

It is significant to note, that President Clinton's signature on the *Apology Resolution* constitutes agreement of the "whereas" facts of the law. Below are excerpts from the *Apology Resolution*, Public Law 103-150, [5] signed by President Bill Clinton on November 23, 1993:

President Clinton signs Public Law 103-150, the "Apology Resolution" to Native Hawaiians, on November 23, 1993. Now, therefore, be it...Resolved by the Senate and House of Representatives of the United States of America in Congress assembled,

Whereas, in a message to Congress on December 18, 1893, President Grover Cleveland reported fully and accurately on the illegal acts of the conspirators, described such acts as an "act of war, committed with the participation of a diplomatic representative of the United States and without authority of Congress", and acknowledged that by such acts the government of a peaceful and friendly people was overthrown...

Whereas, President Cleveland further concluded that a "substantial wrong has thus been done which a due regard for our national character as well as the rights of the injured people requires we should endeavor to repair" and called for the restoration of the Hawaiian monarchy...

Whereas, in pursuance of the conspiracy to overthrow the Government of Hawaii, the United States Minister and the naval representatives of the United States caused armed naval forces of the United States to invade the sovereign Hawaiian nation on January 16, 1893, and to position themselves near the Hawaiian Government buildings and the Iolani Palace to intimidate Queen Liliuokalani and her Government...

The Congress

- apologizes to Native Hawaiians on behalf of the people of the United States for the overthrow of the Kingdom of Hawaii on January 17, 1893... and the deprivation of the rights of Native Hawaiians to self-determination;

- expresses its commitment to acknowledge the ramifications of the overthrow of the Kingdom of Hawaii, in order to provide a proper foundation for reconciliation between the United States and the Native Hawaiian people; and

- urges the President of the United States to also acknowledge the ramifications of the overthrow of the Kingdom of Hawaii and to support reconciliation efforts between the United States and the Native Hawaiian people.

There are two problems with the *Apology Resolution*, which to date, have prevented the full restoration of the Kingdom of Hawai'i and removal of the proxy government of the State of Hawai'i.

The *Apology Resolution* is only addressed to "Native Hawaiians", which has set up the erroneous premise of a "nation within a nation" remedy that is being promoted by the United States government. It is my view, among thousands of people interested in Hawaiian Sovereignty, and especially the view of King Keli'i Silva, that full independence is the only acceptable solution; not divided sovereignty.

Please note, that in part 7, I have included some very informative information regarding **King Keli'i's refusal of the "nation within nation" dialogue**.

You can go to Part 7 and review King Keli'i's writings about settling for "nation within a nation", as well as review the writings of Pearl Means (of the Navajo Nation) about her warning to never settling for "nation within a nation".

The second problem with the *Apology Resolution* is that it does not provide an appropriate remedy equal to the treasonous actions perpetrated upon the Kingdom of Hawai'i. Instead, the *Apology Resolution* promotes the idea of "reconciliation" (rather than "restitution"). See below:

> **... The Congress**
>
> - *expresses its commitment to acknowledge the ramifications of the overthrow of the Kingdom of Hawaii, <u>in order to provide a proper foundation for reconciliation</u> between the United States and the Native Hawaiian people; and*
>
> - *urges the President of the United States to also acknowledge the ramifications of the overthrow of the Kingdom of Hawaii <u>and to support reconciliation efforts</u> between the United States and the Native Hawaiian people."*

"Reconciliation" is not the proper remedy required by the World Court --- instead, "restitution" is required.

THE APPROPRIATE REMEDY FOR TREASON AGAINST THE HAWAIIAN NATION AND QUEEN LILI'UOKALANI IS RESTITUTION, NOT RECONCILIATION

A Word Study of "Restitution"

res·ti·tu·tion
/ˌrestəˈt(y)o͞oSH(ə)n/

noun
noun: restitution

1. the restoration of something lost or stolen to its proper owner.
   "seeking the restitution of land taken from blacks under apartheid"
   synonyms: return, restoration, handing back, surrender
   "restitution of the land seized"

2. recompense for injury or loss.
   "he was ordered to pay $6,000 in restitution"
   synonyms: compensation, recompense, reparation, damages, indemnification, indemnity, reimbursement, repayment, redress, remuneration
   "restitution for the damage caused"

3. the restoration of something to its original state.
   "restitution of the damaged mucosa"

   - PHYSICS
   the resumption of an object's original shape or position through elastic recoil.

Origin

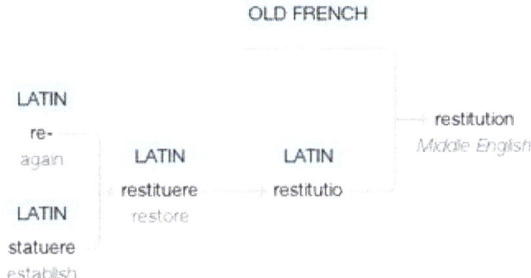

Middle English: from Old French, or from Latin *restitutio(n-)*, from *restituere* 'restore,' from *re-* 'again' + *statuere* 'establish.'

According to Professor Francis Anthony Boyle:[14]

> ... under international law, if you have a violation of this nature, the appropriate remedy is not simply reconciliation, apology or reparations, but restitution. That is, to set right the harm that had been done. To restore the situation to what it had been before the violation in 1893.

Professor Francis A. Boyle Discusses the Appropriate Remedy

Professor Francis A. Boyle explains the appropriate remedy for the U.S. Armed Invasion of the Hawaiian Kingdom in 1893. What follows are excerpts of a speech given by Professor Francis Anthony Boyle on December 28, 1993. [14]

He explains that based on the word, "invasion" (President Cleveland states "armed invasion by the United States"), which is then reiterated in the *Apology Resolution* by the Congress of the United States and signed by President Clinton, that the only remedy is restitution. See excerpts of Professor Boyle's speech below:

> Pursuant to the conspiracy naval representatives called armed forces of the United States to invade the sovereign Hawaiian nation on January 16, 1893, and to position themselves near the Hawaiian government buildings and the ['Iolani] Palace to intimidate the Queen [Liliuokalani] and her government.

Notice the use of the word "invade."... That's what it was, a clearly illegal act, an invasion in violation of treaties and international agreement, an invasion in violation of international law, and the United States Constitution, the overthrow of a lawful government. And again, under international law when you have a violation of treaties of this magnitude, the World Court has ruled that the only appropriate remedy is restitution.

Damages are not enough, reparations are not enough - that is the payment of money - or giving you an island over here and saying, Here, you can have that island." **No, restitution, to restore what you once had, that is the Kingdom of Hawai'i, your independent nation state, this is the appropriate remedy...**

The Proper Remedy of Restoration Is Provided by the King of Hawai'i

Because the *Apology Resolution* did not provide the proper remedy, and the United States government is doing nothing to correct it, **the remedy to fully restore the Kingdom of Hawai'i is now in the hands of King Edmund K. Silva, Jr., which he has been doing for over a decade.**

As King, he heads the Kingdom government, a restored Constitutional Monarchy, which was the form of government that existed at the time of Queen Lili'uokalani's surrender of her Kingdom government to the United States of America.

"I, Liliuokalani, by the Grace of God, and under the Constitution of the Hawaiian Kingdom, Queen, *do hereby solemnly protest against any and all acts done against myself and the constitutional Government of the Hawaiian Kingdom by certain persons claiming to have established a Provisional Government of and for this Kingdom. That I yield to the superior force of the United States of America".*[15]

Part 3
Introducing the King of Hawai'i

ALI'I NUI MŌ'I EDMUND KELI'I SILVA, JR.

Edmund Keli'i Silva, Jr. has taken on the role as Ali'i Nui Mō'i (High Chief, King) of the Kingdom of Hawai'i.[16, 17]

On November 22, 2002, the Prime Minister of the Hawaiian Kingdom, along with the Council of Regency (Na Kupuna Council O' Hawai'i Nei), the Na Kupuna Council Hawai'i Moku of the legislative body of government, and the Royal Kupuna of the House of Nobles, proclaimed King Edmund Keli'i Silva, Jr. as the lawful successor to Ali'i Nui Mō'i (High Chiefs and Kings) of ancient Hawai'i.[3]

King Keli'i has pledged his life to do everything he can to legally restore the Kingdom of Hawai'i to its rightful place among the nations of the world - as a non-aligned nation.

Not an easy role, it could be said that he is taking on the whole world in his role as King, because as I said earlier, the whole world has yet to realize what really happened to the Kingdom of Hawai'i in 1893, and that the Kingdom of Hawai'i is NOT, and never has legally been, the 50th State in the United States.

The Royal Genealogy of King Edmund Keli'i Silva, Jr.

Edmund Keli'i Silva, Jr. comes from the highest royal bloodline, and is widely acknowledged as a man of great intelligence, a man of the highest integrity, a man of peace, a man of destiny and a visionary, who has dedicated his life to improve the Hawaiian Islands and the world through self-sustainability projects and programs.

We have traced his genealogy to King Kamehameha I and King Kamehameha Nui of Mau'i and back into the mists of history; linking him to Hawaiian Royalty...

Per ancient protocol in selecting a King, descendants of the original members of the House of Nobles established by King Kamehameha III, chose Edmund K. Silva, Jr., Ali'i Nui Mo'i, high chief and King of and for the Kingdom of Hawai'i.[59]

Princess Ella Ahyin Kalauokalani Silva-Abe
Royal Genealogist

PER ANCIENT PROTOCOL IN SELECTING A KING, THE HOUSE OF NOBLES WAS ESTABLISHED BY KING KAMEHAMEHA III. DESCENDANTS, WHO ARE THE ORIGINAL MEMBERS OF THE HOUSE OF NOBLES, AND WHOSE FATHERS SAT IN COUNCIL WITH KING KAMEHAMEHA III, CHOSE EDMUND K. SILVA, JR., TO BE ALI'I NUI MO'I, HIGH CHIEF AND KING OF AND FOR, THE KINGDOM OF HAWAI'I.

Queen Liliuokalani in her book, "Hawaii's Story",[19] speaks to the unwritten law of Hawai'i Nei when choosing a chief to rule:

> "Since the king had refused to nominate his successor, the election was with the legislature. It must not be forgotten, however, that the unwritten law of Hawaii Nei required that the greatest chief, or the one having the most direct claim to the throne, must rule. The legislature could not choose from the people at large, but was confined to a decision between rival claimants having an equal or nearly equal relation in the chiefhood to the throne."

Humble in spirit regarding his Kingship, as well as why he was the one chosen rather than other claimants, King Keli'i writes in "Royal Proclamation":[20]

> *We, my Ohana, make no claim of greatness, entitlements, titles, or responsibilities to ourselves based upon pride and the need to have. We are the Royal Priesthood House of Kamehameha nui 'Ai Lu'au [also written Kamehamehanui Ai'luau][21], which is the Royal House of Pi'ilani [22] which is the House of Maui-loa[23] that is the House of Hawai'i-loa [24] that is the House of Kumuhonua [25], the first human of 'Io who is God. We merely recognize our family lineage as pure*

and direct and do not question our responsibilities attendant thereto. Our motives are resigned in faith and our actions empowered in spirit, as were our ancestors, to be accountable on behalf of our lineage to the covenants made by our ancestors on behalf of our people.

We believe that there exists no higher royal lineage of greater calling in Hawai'i. Nevertheless, we refrain disputing other royal claimants who may simultaneously claim responsibility over the resources and welfare of our Native Hawaiian people. However, we present our lineal calling with detailed record and specificity and, in turn, ask for theirs. We would then compare and reconcile the correct levels of responsibilities according to (1) lineage, and (2) competency, skill, and capacity. That is the way of our traditional cultural protocols of ancient governance. We publicly proclaim our preeminent royal Hawaiian lineage.

We proclaim Concomitant skills and mastery in the most ancient Native Hawaiian cultural practices of royal Governance (laws of consecration and Ohana servitude), the 12 levels of the practice of kahuna Nui specifically that of prophecy and healing arts, and the cultural mastery of ancient traditional justice (kukakuka – ho'oponopono).

King Kamehameha I & King Keli'i

In this, we give testimony and bear witness that ours is not only the working knowledge, but also, the mastery of all the skills and capability likewise evident by personal exhibitions and proof of qualified formal training even documented by disinterested third parties.

Our vision is based upon uncommon competencies originating from the highest and most respected royal lineage in the known history of the Kingdom of Hawai'i. Our vision is also based upon specific competencies originating prior to 1100 AD - the time of the reformation of the Hawaiian archipelago's system of governance into today's familiar "Ali'i System." Too, our vision incorporates the competencies originating from three major ancient voyages settling the American continents and Polynesia.

Although we do not claim preeminent royalty throughout history, we do claim having the highest priesthood and royal lineage concerning the Hawaiian archipelago from 387 AD to present.

We believe that there is no other prospective Hawaiian claimant or family that can make and document their ancient genealogical rights comparative to ours."

In addition to the genealogical information just presented, King Keli'i Silva provided a more detailed genealogy in a letter to Governor David Ige of Hawaii, linking it to Hawaiian Royalty from the year 387 AD. [26]

I am taking this opportunity to lawfully state with clarity of mind, that I have Hawaiian Royal Family buried on Mauna a Wākea. [27, 28] *Also too, legend has it, that King Kamehameha the great is possibly buried there as well. My mother who is 83 years of age and dad who is 85 (Both living) are direct heirs to the Kamehameha line and the sacred royal line called "Ni'au pi'o"* [29] *(Hawai'i's sacred royal child) of highest rank and divine lineage.*

My Grandmother Kalanikauika'alaneo Kai Keōpūolani-Ahu-i-Kekai-Makuahine-a-Kama-Kalani-Kau-i-Kealaneo (1778–1823)[30] *was the highest ranking wife of King Kamehameha I, and of the "Ni'au pi'o" (Hawai'i's sacred royal child) blood line. This is my sacred Blood Line that is undisputed, sacred and divine. I am "Ni'au pi'o" (Hawai'i's sacred royal child). We are the Royal Priesthood House of Kamehameha Nui 'Ai Lu'au* [21] *which is the Royal House of Pi'ilani* [22] *which is the House of Maui-loa* [23] *that is the House of Hawai`i-loa* [24] *that is the House of Kumuhonua,* [25] *the first human of 'Io, who is God.*

My family has publicly proclaimed our preeminent royal Hawaiian lineage. We proclaim concomitant skills and mastery in the most ancient Native Hawaiian cultural practices of royal governance (laws of consecration and ohana servitude), the 12 levels of the practice of kahuna nui specifically that of prophecy and healing arts, and the cultural mastery of ancient traditional justice (kūkākūkā – ho`oponopono).

In this, we give testimony and bear witness that ours is not only the working knowledge, but also, the mastery of all the skills and capability likewise evident by personal exhibitions and proof of qualified formal training even documented by disinterested third parties. Our vision is based upon uncommon competencies originating from the highest and most respected royal lineage in the known history of the Kingdom of Hawai`i. Our vision is also based upon specific competencies originating prior to 1100 AD - the time of the reformation of the Hawaiian archipelago's system of governance into today's familiar "Ali'i System."

...Our lineage is also popularly known as that of King Kekaulike,[31] the King of Maui and the father of Kamehameha Nui 'Ai Lu'au. Maui Kingdom was ancient Hawai`i's most powerful and significant Kingdom. It comprised the most divine royal lineage whose origins derived from the most ancient birthrights from Oahu and Kaua'i. Our royal genealogical record was that ancient oral chant kept and added upon, throughout the millennia and through the voyages of our ancestors into the Pacific to settle the uninhabited islands.

The ancient Hawaiians had no written language and all records were oral chants. Our lineage was kept by specific priesthood holders and solemnly recited in Royal Courts of the Kingdoms of Maui, Hawai'i, Oahu and Kauai. Our record was put into writing by the royal genealogist, Hoku Pakipika, shortly after the birth of the sacred High Chief of highest rank, Kapahupinea-Kaleikoa-Keopuhiwa-Paki, on February 14, 1871 in order to protect Hawaii's highest royal birthright. At that time, Kamehameha V was Hawai'i's king and the last of the Kamehameha I dynasty, which was of lower lineage to Kamehameha Nui 'Ai Lu'au. The two royal heirs of Kamehameha I had additional lineage to the High Chiefs Kalola, daughter of King Kekaulike, but the mere younger sister of King Kamehameha Nui 'Ai Lu'au.

GROWING RECOGNITION OF KING EDMUND KELI'I SILVA, JR.

Lamaku Mikahala Roy

There are people throughout Hawai'i [32] and all over the world, who endorse King Edmund K. Silva, Jr. as the rightful King of Hawai'i. Lamaku Mikahala Roy - Kahu, Ahu'ena Heiau Kamakahonu, Hawai'i, wrote a letter endorsing Edmund K. Silva, Jr. as Ali'i Nui Mō'i (High Chief/King), as seen in this excerpt:[33]

Alii Nui Mo'i Edmund K. Silva, Jr. by the support matrix of the people, Nou Ke Akua Ke Aupuni Hawaii, has demonstrated commitment and consistent love for Hawaii.

There is no other that has demonstrated commitment and consistent love for Hawaii.

There is no other that has demonstrated this level of love and dedication. His reach of concern begins at our beginnings ~ in the spirituality of our Lands. He defends Mauna a Wakea in the now ~ and for years (visible by website contributions) he has consistently been the voice and presence of protection of all life within sacred Hawaii from ka Moku o Keawe through Papahanaoumokuakea. It is His Voice that been the voice echoing in the halls that would pose potential or actual threat to Hawaii. It is His Presence that is known by leaders in the U.S., Hawaii and the world.

Pearl Means

Another significant endorsement comes from **Pearl Means, of the Navajo Nation**. Pearl's late husband was the well-known leader, Russell Means,[34,35] who vigilantly led the fight to counteract the continued destruction and decimation of his Native American brothers and sisters by the lies and actions of the American Government.

IN A RECENT LETTER, PEARL MEANS CALLED FOR INDIGENOUS PEOPLE ALL OVER THE WORLD TO STAND IN SOLIDARITY WITH KING KELI'I, AND FOR HAWAIIAN SOVEREIGNTY.[36]

Ya'at'eeh my Relatives, Friends and Allies:

With great concerns, I speak to you, the sacred geometry is aligned and the time is now. ***I am calling upon Indian Country, all Indigenous Peoples from all over the earth, World Leaders and Nations*** *to stand with me, and the Navajo Nation in support of the King, Ali'i Nui Mo'i Edmund Keli'i Silva, Jr., of the Kingdom of Hawai'i and its people towards freedom with Full restoration and independence of their Nation.*

98 Year Old Kupuna, Auntie Ku'uipo (Ipo) Kanehele of Maui Island

"Recently, I met him. Even our ancestors would approve of him. In - fact they guided me to him. He is a man of courage and conviction. He is dedicated to the truth and loves unconditionally. **I found him to be unselfish, brave, wise, strong and compassionate. He stands for justice and a sovereign Hawai'i. His plans are visionary and pono.** I wish I could live long enough to see it all come into being because it is.

He is not a group. He is Hawai'i. He is you and we are him. We are one nation, one voice and one people. In times past, there have been many who made strong claims that they are the one's chosen to be king, queen, regent or prime minister of and for the Kingdom of Hawai'i and watched them fall. They took bribes, threaten to be put in prison, harassed and scared off by the Federal and State Governmental agencies of the United States. Worse yet, our own Kanaka maoli (people) worked evil against them.

Let me introduce to you our warrior of light ordained by Akua. His God given name is Edmund Keli'i Silva, Jr." [75] *I continue to sound the kahea to unite as one voice, one people and one nation. Come together under the flag of our Ali'i Nui Mo'i Keli'i (Edmund K. Silva Jr.) He will lead us to victory. For I have heard Akua and Akua is faithful. Blessed be the name of Akua and blessings to our Mo'i and, our Kingdom of Hawai'i Nei.*[76]

MOVING THE KINGDOM FORWARD

King Keli'i Offers an Invitation to Unite as One People

At the end of the video of King Keli'i's Speech, [37] you will see his invitation to "Come Sit, Unite as One People, and Determine the Future Together". He also reminds us that "the Kingdom Path is the Path of Aloha".

Come in, come sit, eat and talk...

Go Forward. The time is now!

The power is you! We are awake! We want a better world!

Together, we can determine our future.

We can consciously choose to build a civilization that is sustainable, self-reliant, unified, and at peace.

We, as people, know what needs to be done.

We are dissolving the power of the past, by reorganizing our Civilization on this planet.

The Kingdom of Hawai'i is restored as a beacon of light,

Showing the way to a new civilization based on respect for all members of the Human Family.

A civilization where everyone is informed, through open communications, and participates through truly democratic processes.

Let us work with humbleness as one 'People',

In celebrating the need to live in "Oneness" and the spirit of aloha.

Together, let us build a civilization that hears the voices of all the innocent creatures on the Earth.

A civilization that lives in harmony with the ecological systems that support us.

The Kingdom Path is the Path of Aloha,

A love for all creation, and a belief, that we can create

What we know in our hearts is the highest expression of who we are as a species.

Come! Join us in creating and celebrating the new civilization.

Our goal is to create a model of peace and prosperity for the Human Family, in harmony with the natural world and our planet.

E pili mau na pomaika'i aia 'oe- May blessings ever be with you.

The Kingdom of Hawai'i is restored, and I am the King.

Humbly, I address, Ancestors who have passed on.

Now, you are the iwi Kupuna cherished by ourselves, your descendants. You passed on in faith that the Hawaiian Kingdom would be restored.

You trusted in Akua for the restoration of the Kingdom of Hawai'i.

Rest in the sacred peace of Akua.

From the past through the present, I greatly thank each one of you who sacrificed life, health, and earthly belongings to restore the Kingdom of Hawai'i.

I thank those non-Kanaka Maoli supporters who believed along with us. You endured ridicule for your willingness to help us.

I am most grateful for the great work of all the people in the groups formed to help us, the Hawaiian people.

Now, let us unite as one.

SEEKING THE PATH OF ALOHA

A Different Sort of King

IT IS APPARENT TO ME THAT KING EDMUND KELI'I SILVA, JR. IS A DIFFERENT SORT OF KING; SOME CALL HIM FRIEND, SOME CALL HIM WARRIOR, SOME CALL HIM PEACEMAKER, AND MOST WHO ACTUALLY KNOW HIM, CALL HIM, ENLIGHTENED.

In 2014, the King wrote to United Nations Secretary General Ban Ki-moon, the letter "The Kingdom of Hawai'i Independence". In this letter, he speaks from his heart about "love": [60]

> *To the nations of the world, I write to you not as a King to rule but as a King who empowers his people with love, education, prosperity and freedom.* **In our journey united in love there will be many changes to right that which is wrong, create light to replace darkness, and rewrite or remove that which segregates, enslaves or destroys the spiritual essence of our birthright.**
>
> *I write to transmit love to each of you, for love, will speak to your essence. It is that sacred place within that tells you what you are doing is right.*
>
> *In the case of the Kingdom of Hawai'i, doing right is no more than is called for by the United Nations Declaration on the Granting of Independence to Colonial Countries and Peoples...*

His leadership style is glimpsed throughout the letter, "Peaceful End". [38] Here are some excerpts:

> *A foundational question to be answered by all parties is whether there is one Human Family or not. If any party believes that the answer to that question is "no," then what divisions does that party claim transcend the unity of our species? Religion? Race? Nation? Tribe? Culture? A conscious Human knows that these are all artificial divisions. Those who would divide the Human family in such a way are preaching a lie!*
>
> *Making Peace. Any ass can start a war. A peacemaker requires patience, intelligence, empathy, and creativity. Those who are parties to the conflict have a conflict of interest in the outcome. Political leaders feel compelled to take positions popular with their followers, whether those positions lead to peace or not.*
>
> **...*The Future.***
>
> *What is peace? Peace is mutual respect for diverse practices and beliefs and the freedom to choose one's own path. Peace exists when people are happy and living in harmony with each other and with the rest of the Natural World. Now is the time to decide on the Human Future. The pathways are clearly laid out before us. We can choose to rise above our bloody history and create a world in which the happiness of all and harmony with Nature is the goal.*

We can continue to live in a heightened state of fear and stress with the constant threat of conflict for more generations. We can light the fuse and blow up everything.

Will homo sapiens mean knowledgeable Humans, who never progressed beyond the limitations of their historical programming, or wise Humans, who saw the abyss and turned down a different path to truly evolve towards their highest potential?

The Kingdom is prepared to assist in any way possible to bend the arc of history towards peace.

In another letter, "Coming Together in Peace", the King speaks about the Human family. He states... "We are 'Ohana family."[39]

It has been said by our ancestors, Old Men and Mothers know the folly of war. Leaders are bestowed with the responsibility of making decisions based on sustaining a minimum of the next seven generations. We are at a fragile time in our human experience. With wise leadership great things can emerge for all of humanity and our earth.

Let history recount this time as a great time of change, hope and a time of evolution. As allies and world leaders, we have the strength to do what is right and noble for our nations, neighbors, the entire human family, and the natural world. Standing alone we will perish.

Huna Sacred Moral values of 'ohana' family:

1. Treat the earth and all that dwells upon her with respect.

2. Remain close to the Great Spirit – Akua.

3. Show great respect for your fellow beings and the natural world.

4. Work together for the benefit of all humankind and the natural world.

5. Give assistance and kindness wherever needed and do it with unconditional love.

6. Do what you know to be right all the time, even if you're standing alone.

7. Look after the well-being of mind and body so that you are not corruptible.

8. Dedicate a share of your efforts to the greater good of all.

9. Be truthful and honest at all times. It is better to hear an uncomfortable truth than a lie.

10. Take full responsibility for your actions with courage and respect for self.

Gentlemen, your nation are family that we call 'Ohana... There are no citizens, subjects or friends...

We are 'Ohana family.

'Ohana is family. Our 'Ohana includes those we have always known as our family, surrounding us with love at the time of our birth. However 'Ohana also includes those we choose to call our family, for the connection we share with them enriches our life. 'Ohana becomes a sacred form for sharing our lives with Aloha, for it gives us the unconditional gifts of love, understanding, forgiving, and acceptance.

'Ohana is the most secure and comfort-filled support we have for facing truth, for 'Ohana never loses hope. The bonds of 'Ohana are strong yet supple: They flex with giving and with the love and acceptance of Aloha, yet they are made rigidly secure by those same supports. These bonds may be tested, but they cannot be broken. 'Ohana is a human circle of complete Aloha.

A Study of Plato's Philosopher Kings & the Ship of State Metaphor

LIKE PLATO'S PHILOSOPHER KINGS, KING KELI'I SILVA SEEKS JUSTICE, AND THE GREATEST GOOD FOR ALL THE HUMAN FAMILY AND THE NATURAL WORLD.

It might be helpful to study Book VI of "The Republic" by the ancient philospher, Plato, to fully understand what is different about the kingship of Edmund K. Silva, Jr.

In his masterpiece dialogue, Plato presents us with Socrates (who speaks in the first person) as he is retelling a discussion on the nature of "justice", and the "form of the good" (some feel that "the form of the good" means balance and harmony within oneself, which is then projected outward into the physical world). This discussion uses the metaphor of a Utopian Kalipolis (his ideal city-sate). Plato teaches Socrates what would be required for an ideal city-state to exist by way of the metaphor, "Ship of State". Plato concludes the discussion of justice and the form of good with this: 40

"IF AN IDEAL CITY-STATE IS TO EVER COME INTO BEING, PHILOSOPHERS [MUST] BECOME KINGS... OR THOSE NOW CALLED KINGS [MUST] ...GENUINELY AND ADEQUATELY PHILOSOPHIZE" (THE REPUBLIC, 5.473D).

Plato Teaches that a Philosopher Should Be the Navigator of the Ship of State

An entry from Wikipedia clarifies the meaning of the Plato's metaphor, "Ship of State": 41

In the metaphor Plato describes the steering of a ship as just like any other "craft" or profession - in particular, that of a statesman. He then runs the metaphor in reference to a particular type of government: democracy. Plato's democracy is not the modern notion of a mix of democracy and republicanism, but rather direct democracy by way of pure majority rule.In the metaphor, found at 488a-489d, Plato's Socrates compares the population at large to a strong but nearsighted ship owner, whose knowledge of seafaring is lacking. The quarreling sailors are demagogues and politicians, and the ship's navigator, a stargazer, is the philosopher.The sailors flatter themselves with claims to knowledge of sailing, though they know nothing of navigation, and are constantly vying with one another for the approval of the ship owner so to captain the ship, going so far as to stupefy the ship owner with drugs and wine. Meanwhile, they dismiss the navigator as a useless stargazer, though he is the only one with adequate knowledge to direct the ship's course.

Plato's Philosopher King

Socrates' answer is known as "the paradox of the philosopher king"[42] and is stated dramatically at 473d: the way to bring about a just state is to have it ruled by philosophers, or what is commonly called "the Philosopher-King. [40]

"This conclusion would naturally be felt as contradictory by most of Socrates' listeners, because at that time (as well as today), philosophers were perceived as people with "their heads in the clouds" and consequently, unfit for politics. So now, to defend his view, Socrates must finally tell us what he means by the ideal, perfect "philosopher" and what sort of education would produce such a person.

UNTIL PHILOSOPHERS RULE AS KINGS, OR THOSE WHO ARE NOW CALLED KINGS AND LEADING MEN, GENUINELY AND ADEQUATELY PHILOSOPHIZE, THAT IS, UNTIL POLITICAL POWER AND PHILOSOPHY ENTIRELY COINCIDE... CITIES WILL HAVE NO REST FROM EVILS... THERE CAN BE NO HAPPINESS, EITHER PUBLIC OR PRIVATE, IN ANY OTHER CITY.

Thus, the emphasis in the Platonic notion of the philosopher king lies more on the first word than the second. While relying on conventional Greek contrasts between king and tyrant and between the king as individual ruler and the multitudinous rule of aristocracy and democracy; Plato makes little use of the notion of kingship per se.

That he had used the word, however, was the key to the later career of the notion in imperial Rome and monarchical Europe. To the Stoic Roman emperor Marcus Aurelius [44] *(reigned 161–180), what mattered was that even kings should be philosophers, rather than that only philosophers should rule."*

I am sure you understand the reason that I am bringing up the topic of a Plato's Philosopher King. By doing so in this book, I am suggesting that what is different about King Keli'i is his tendency to lead / govern the way that Plato has described his "Philosopher Kings" to rule. It is my opinion that King Keli'i exhibits not only the same character traits, but he has consistently shown his desire is to provide freedom, justice and the greatest good for the people, and the land of Hawai'i Nei.

Do I believe that King Keli'i Silva represents what Plato has described as a Philosopher King? Yes, I do. In the future, we will certainly know whether or not this is true of King Keli'i.

A Poem for King Edmund Keli'i Silva, Jr.
Philosopher King

A Student of Life, Listener of Spirit.

This is the man, Edmund Keli'i Silva, Jr.

When people say the word, "King", they think, I don't want a King! A King looks down on the people from his thrown.

Not so, with King Keli'i. He is a King, yes, but he is a King who sits NOT on a throne, but sits among his people – giving all, and taking little.

Not embracing "the divine right of kings"; instead, embracing a "divine calling" to serve God for the greater good.

He seeks justice, righteousness, wisdom and truth, so that he is able to care for ALL of life on this planet.

He is unafraid and courageous; a protector, philosopher, friend, teacher and student.

He is Gentle, Kind and Steadfast.

A Warrior ~ of Peace, of Light, of Mission, of Aloha.

He said yes, "I will". Through sacrifice, heartache and deprivation, he serves … with joy and a humble heart.

Alie James

Part 4
The Kingdom is Restored
by King Edmund Keli'i Silva, Jr.

KINGDOM RESTORATION

The Montevideo Convention Supports Kingdom Restoration

The basis for Kingdom Restoration lies in the Montevideo Convention on the Rights and Duties of States, a treaty signed at Montevideo, Uruguay, on December 26, 1933, during the Seventh International Conference of American States. The Convention codified the declarative theory of statehood as accepted as part of customary international law. [45] In the *Montevideo Convention on the Rights and Duties of States*, the definition of a State is found in Article 1.

Article 1: The state as a person of international law should possess the following qualifications: a) a permanent population; b) a defined territory; c) government; and d) capacity to enter into relations with the other states.

King Keli'i Silva states, "Satisfying these four criteria gives me the legal authority to restore and rebuild the Kingdom of Hawai'i Government. I formally separated the Kingdom from the United States through a Declaration issued on June 23, 2003".[20]

The King Discusses the Illegal Overthrow of the Hawaiian Kingdom in a Letter to Governor David Ige

In the letter, "Moving Forward", [47] King Keli'i tells Governor Ige: "Despite the unprovoked and unfortunate invasion and illegal overthrow of my government so well documented since 1893, we have never given up our rights so eloquently stated by my cousin." In addition to that statement, the King also cited in the letter to the Governor, Queen Lili'uokalani's protest:

> *"I, Lili'uokalani, by the Grace of God, and under the Constitution of the Hawaiian Kingdom, Queen, do hereby solemnly protest against any and all acts done against myself and the constitutional Government of the Hawaiian Kingdom by certain persons claiming to have established a Provisional Government of and for this Kingdom. That I yield to the superior force of the United States of America whose Minister Plenipotentiary, His Excellency John L. Stevens, has caused United States troops to be landed at Honolulu and declared that he would support the said Provisional Government. Now to avoid any collision of armed forces, and perhaps the loss of life, I do this under protest, and impelled by said force yield my authority until such time as the Government of the United States shall, upon facts being presented to it, undo the action of its representative and reinstate me in the authority which I claim as the constitutional sovereign of the Hawaiian Islands."*

King Keli'i further clarifies his position to Governor Ige:

My cousin yielded her authority to the U.S. under a condition, "yield my authority UNTIL such time as the Government of the United States shall, upon facts being presented to it undo the action of its representative."

Following the forcible acquisition of the Kingdom of Hawai'i and the geopolitical shadows cast upon the Hawaiian Islands, the United States of America declared that all previous treaties concluded between the Kingdom of Hawai'i and nation-states, such as the Treaty of Friendship, Commerce and Navigation weres null and void.

The United States does not speak for my Kingdom. My ancestors never acknowledged any cancellation of treaties with you and neither have I. Therefore as the Constitutional King, I declare and up-hold the rule of law and equity that you are ethically, morally, emotionally and spiritually connected to me for all perpetuity."

The United States Offers No Justice or Remedy; Yet the Kingdom of Hawai'i is Restored

To date, it is apparent that no justice or proper remedy will be forthcoming from the United States, as Queen Lili'uokalani so fervently believed would happen at the time of her surrender.

Although not visible, the Kingdom of Hawai'i remained in the hearts and minds of most of the Hawaiian people from the moment of the Queen's surrender. So, as was true for over a century, the Kingdom of Hawai'i was never abolished, and still exists to this day.

In an interview, Ali'i Mana'o Nui Lanny Sinkin stated: [64]

There has been a movement to restore the Hawaiian nation since 1893... it's been a 120 year political movement to reclaim the nation of Hawai'i.

At the time of the overthrow, Hawaii had treaties with major nations across the globe, and those treaties have never been relinquished by the Hawaiian people, the claims to their nation have never been relinquished, the claims to their lands have never been relinquished, they basically consider themselves to be an occupied nation trying to liberate itself and rejoin the community of nations.

The Kingdom of Hawai'i is being restored, reclaimed and reintroduced to the nations of the world through the efforts of the Queen Lili'uokalani's cousin, Ali'i Nui Mō'i Edmund Keli'i Silva, Jr., who is assisted by the hard work of the people in his government. All documentation of the restoration can be found on the Kingdom of Hawai'i's website, http://www.kingdomofhawaii.info.

Also, a special report, "Rebuilding the Government of the Hawaiian Kingdom", [48] can be reviewed for specific details.

King Keli'i Creates a Plan to Restore the Kingdom of Hawai'i Into a Thriving, Sustainable Nation

Recently, the King explained in a Questions & Answers Communique about his vision of a restored Kingdom: [66]

> *That we are a Nation that is reliant upon ourselves, self-sustainable and a nation that lives in harmony with nature and Nature's God. We shall enter into Treaties with other nations that will make sense for Hawai`i.*
>
> *We shall be a non-aligned nation. We shall promote peace and create a Peace Center here in these islands for the Nations of the World to come talk story openly about taking care of their nations through peaceful solutions that are in harmony with the Spirit of Aloha and the lands they live on.*

I suggest that you view the King's Speech Video, [49] and you will notice the consistency in his message. **He shares his vision for Hawai'i, as a thriving, sustainable, non-aligned nation.** The vision he describes has been turned into a Kingdom document called, the *Aloha Aina Project,*[50,54] which is fully discussed in Part 7.

The Constitutional Monarchy Explained

The King Explains the Constitutional Monarchy:[66]

There will be checks and balances, for no kings are dictators. The King represents his people, even at the cost of his own life. History paints kings as ruthless and evil. Myself, I don't hold to that way of governance. My ancestors did not govern with ruthless behavior either. There was however strong superstitious beliefs long before other nations came to these islands that I will not restore.

I believe in free enterprise and free will thinking that all of mankind is free in body and spirit and that women shall be treated with the greatest respect and equal in this Kingdom.

I do not support what I would call "suicide capitalism," where everything that can produce a profit is legitimate, even if it means destroying the ecosystems that support life and Human civilization through climate chaos.

I love education and will promote education that serves our nation's economical and spiritual growth. I believe in science and that there is a way to rid our bodies of all forms of sicknesses and diseases that plague the health and well-being of mankind.

The Kingdom will find solutions for the benefit of this Kingdom and all of mankind, so that we can live a fruitful and meaningful life that is our natural gift, given to us from God. I also believe that the Kingdom can find a solution to heal our earth, i.e. lands, oceans, rivers, forests, from the greed of evil. I look forward to seeing this reversal in my life time.

The King was asked if people living in the Kingdom would be expected to bow down to him, or call him "His Majesty": [66]

Respect is earned; I shall earn the respect of our people. I alone cannot build this nation on my own. I need the people to help me, for together we will build a nation that other nations can emulate. Respectfully, we are all sovereigns and that is how I will walk amongst our people. I will lead by example that others may follow. For in all truth, we all belong to the human family as one.

The King's shares his view about a Constitutional Monarchy having the best chance to be a righteous government in a recent letter, "Establishing Our Government". [51] He writes:

The Kingdom of Hawai'i is Here...

The Kingdom of Hawai'i has evolved throughout the centuries, and is here, now. What may seem new today has at its foundation the governmental structures that existed at the time of my cousin, Queen Lili'uokalani.

Questions have arisen throughout the Kingdom about the Monarchical form of government (which existed at the time of Queen Lili'uokalani's overthrow) and whether or not a Monarchy can be a righteous government?

My answer is yes, and in this letter, I'll discuss reasons why I believe that the unity, strength and longevity of our Kingdom are best served by having a Monarchy. Righteousness will follow suit as we restore the Kingdom with governmental structures that provide protection and the greatest good to all the people and land of Hawai'i.

Knowing now that the King believes that having a Constitutional Monarchy is the best form of government (and is actually a requirement to restore the Kingdom), **it is significant to note that he made it known from the very beginning, that ultimately it becomes the people's choice whether or not they wish the Kingdom of Hawai'i to remain a Constitutional Monarchy. He states:** [51]

In 1893, our kingdom was a kingdom when it was stolen. Today, I am restoring that which was unlawfully taken. Once we are restored and recognized among the nations of the world, I will open the doors for the people to decide what kind of government they want. Until such time, I remain faithful to our Aina, our culture, our traditions, our ancestors, to each of you, and most of all, to Akua.

Keli'i Silva October 21, 2004

The Flag of the Kingdom of Hawai'i

From the lessons learned from the *Kumu Lipo* and from the illegal overthrow of the Hawaiian Kingdom, King Edmund Keli'i Silva, Jr., and those working alongside of him, created the Nation's National Flag. The Kingdom's Flag is explained on the Kingdom of Hawai'i's website. [52]

Ka Hae Hawai'i Aloha o Ke Au Lama
The Beloved Flag of Hawai'i in the Era of Light

A Vision of the Kalo Plant

The Kalo Plant (taro plant) conveys the Spirit of the Kumu Lipo (Creation Chant), which is a two thousand line creation chant. The Kumu Lipo or source of life is an ancient Hawaiian chant, consisting of 2,077 lines traditionally chanted by one person over six hours. The Kumu Lipo chant records the sequence of creation of the aumakua (ancestral-family spirits) and, the Kumu Lipo design shows the sequence of the formation of the universe, leading to what physicists now call the 'Big Bang'.

It reflects the theories about the origins of the cosmos and life on this planet and provides a concept of world order... reminding all of us about the core relationship people have with earth and how to live harmoniously.

The Kumu Lipo is the inspiration that stimulated our spiritual vision for our Nation's flag. The dark blue background behind the 'Kalo' represents the 'po' or the great unknown. Out of the great unknown have emerged our people. Hence the logic of replacing the deep black color respectfully associated to the 'po' as the great unknown with the dark blue establishing our presence. As a resilient people, Hawaiians have never given up our God given right to be a 'Sovereign Kingdom'. Today, based on the lessons of the Kumu Lipo and the lessons of the illegal overthrow of our Kingdom, we have restored our Nation among the nations of the world; and created our Nation's National Flag.

Hō'ili'ili Nani
The Gathering of Beautiful Things, or Restoring What was Taken

King Keli'i recently declared to the Nations of the World, a Resolution, from the Kingdom of Hawai'i.

Although this Resolution was created by the Kingdom to assert the ownership of all lands in the Archipelago belonging to the Crown and Government prior to the illegal overthrow of the Kingdom Government, I believe this document stands as one of the most comprehensive and truthful, historical overviews of Hawaiian history to date.

TO THE NATIONS OF THE WORLD
FROM THE KINGDOM OF HAWAI'I

RESOLUTION

Hō'ili'ili Nani — The Gathering of Beautiful Things or, Restoring What was Taken

Whereas the Hawaiian Archipelago is the spiritual and physical home of the Spirit of Aloha, embodied in the Hawaiian population of the Archipelago; and

Whereas the Hawaiian Archipelago is the ancestral home of the Hawaiian people; and

Whereas the Hawaiian people welcomed foreigners to join the Hawaiian civilization; and

Whereas the Hawaiian people adopted practices of the foreigners, such as transitioning from a traditional governing structure composed of the kuleana of Kahuna, Ali'i, and Maka'āinana to a constitutional monarchy form of government; and

Whereas that constitutional monarchy had treaties with seventeen nations, including the United States, recognizing the Kingdom as a sovereign government; and

Whereas the Kingdom was included within the Universal Postal Union; and

Whereas some among those foreigners lusted after the physical resources and labor that the Hawaiian people could provide; and

Whereas those same foreigners sought to destroy the Hawaiian civilization altogether through suppression of the traditional faith, outlawing spiritual practices, banning cultural practices, displacing Hawaiians from their own lands, banning the Hawaiian language from the schools, and otherwise conducting a campaign of genocide, see United Nations Convention on the Prevention and Punishment of the

Crime of Genocide, adopted by Resolution 263 (III) A of the United Nations General Assembly on December 9, 1948; and
Whereas the ultimate goal of this campaign of genocide was the annexation of the Kingdom of Hawaii into the United States; and

Whereas the United States Minister to the Kingdom conspired with traitorous foreign land holders, businessmen, missionaries and others to seize Queen Liliu'okalani and set in motion such an annexation; and

Whereas a Committee of Safety, composed of fifteen traitors, set in motion the overthrow of the Kingdom Government; and

Whereas the United States Minister to the Kingdom landed United States Marines with Gatling guns and cannon to support the traitors; and

Whereas the United States Minister immediately recognized the illegal Provisional Government formed by the traitors; and

Whereas the traitors coerced the Queen into abdicating her throne by threatening harm to the Queen and her subjects; and

Whereas the Queen called upon the United States Government to restore her to her throne; and

Whereas the United States President acknowledged that the participation of the United States Minister and United States armed forces was an act of war in violation of the treaty of peace between the Kingdom and the United States; and

Whereas the United States President sent a message to the traitors telling them to restore the Queen and the legitimate government, and

Whereas the traitors refused to restore the legitimate government, and

Whereas the United States failed to take the actions necessary to restore the legitimate Kingdom Government; and

Whereas all United States attempts at annexation through treaty failed to receive the constitutionally-required support from the United States Senate; and

Whereas substituting the so-called Newlands Resolution passed in 1898 for a ratified treaty was legally ineffective, such that annexation never took place; and

Whereas the United Nations General Assembly placed Hawai'i on the United Nations list of Non-Self-Governing Territories in 1946; and

Whereas the United States conducted a so-called statehood referendum in 1959 in a manner that violated international law by omitting independence as an option; and

Whereas the United States requested the United Nations remove Hawai'i from the list of Non-Self-Governing Territories claiming Hawai'i had become a state based on the illegal statehood referendum; and

Whereas the United Nations accepted the United States request to remove Hawai'i from the list despite the illegal nature of the statehood referendum; and

Whereas the United States Government recognized the role the United States played in the illegal overthrow of the Kingdom Government in a resolution passed by the United States Congress, Public Law 103-150, and signed by President Clinton in 1993; and

Whereas lawfully the Kingdom never ceased to exist; and

Whereas the Kingdom Government was restored through the creation of a government through the traditional method of convening Kupuna; and

Whereas the Kingdom Government issued a Proclamation announcing the formation of the Government, adopted the 1837 Constitution of the Kingdom, and selected as Ali'i Nui Mō'ī (High Chief/King) Edmund Keli'i Nalikolauokalani Silva, Jr., whose lineage traces back to Queen Liliu'okalani, King Kamehameha I, and Kamehameha nui 'Ai Lu'au; and

Whereas the King issued a Declaration of Independence reclaiming the Kingdom's right to sovereignty; and

Whereas the King has put into place all necessary officials to conduct governance; and

Whereas the Kingdom Government has performed acts of governance documented on the Kingdom website at www.KingdomofHawaii.info; and

Whereas such acts of governance are sufficient to satisfy international requirements for a government to be recognized, as set forth in the Montevideo Treaty; and

Whereas the Kingdom Government continues its restoration process; and

Whereas a key element in that restoration is the return of all lands seized by foreign powers through aiding and abetting treason, enacting a legally ineffective resolution pretending to annex the Kingdom, conducting an alleged statehood referendum that violated international law, and otherwise acting illegally to steal the lands of the Kingdom; and

Whereas the Kingdom desires to reestablish its full sovereignty through a peaceful transition back to the governing structure that existed prior to the illegal acts noted above with the subjects of the restored Kingdom then free to adopt whatever form of government best suits the goal of reestablishing a self-sufficient, self-reliant, non-aligned nation, preserving and enhancing the traditional Hawaiian civilization, adopting modern practices not inconsistent with the traditional civilization, and otherwise restoring nationhood to the Hawaiian Archipelago;

Now, Therefore Be It Resolved, that the Kingdom of Hawai'i reclaims all lands belonging to the Kingdom prior to 1893; and

Be It Further Resolved that all currently unused lands that once belonged to the Kingdom will be made available to the people to raise healthy food, restore endangered species, gather materials necessary for cultural and spiritual purposes, establish/reestablish sacred sites, and otherwise reconnect the people with the 'Aina and each other in the Spirit of Aloha; and

Be It Further Resolved that the Kingdom hereby demands that all revenues currently flowing to the foreign governmental entities from Kingdom lands be delivered henceforth to the Kingdom; and

Be It Further Resolved that the Kingdom considers the United States and its subdivisions, such as the State of Hawai'i, to owe reparations to the Kingdom for all funds derived from Kingdom lands and other Kingdom resources, misappropriated by the such governments, plus a suitable interest on those funds; and

Be it Further Resolved that all nations having treaties with the Hawaiian Kingdom and their contemporary freed colonies or subdivisions, who are subject to obligations to these treaties of friendship, work to support justice in the Pacific; and

Be It Further Resolved that the Kingdom calls upon all foreign nations, particularly those nations having treaties with the Kingdom prior to the above-noted illegal internal acts of treason and external act of war, for support, solidarity, and recognition.

Resolved this 22 day of 2016.

_____/s/_____
Edmund Keli'i Silva Jr.
Ali'i Nui Mōi (High Chief/King)

_____/s/_____
Edmund Keli'i Silva, Sr.
Direct Descendent to King Kamehameha Ai Lu'au
Congress - Na Kupuna Council O Hawai'i Nei
Royal House of Nobles

_____/s/_____
Princess Ella Ayhing Kalauokalani Abe-Silva
Royal Genealogist

_____/s/_____
Princess Chystal Opu'uokalani Naki-Silva
Royal Historian

_____/s/_____
Kahuna Palani Tamehameha Kamehaloha Anuumealani Nobriga
Temple of Lono

_____/s/_____
Jennifer Pawlowski
Chief Justice
Kingdom Supreme Court

_____/s/_____
Lanny Alan Sinkin
Ali'i Mana'o Nui (Chief Advocate)

_____/s/_____
Mikahala Roy
First Citizen

_____/s/_____
Kai Landow
Minister of Foreign Relations

_____/s/_____
Terra 'Aina Blackford
Coordinator of Program Development

_____/s/_____
Bradley L. Duell, Ph.D (Kauilapele)
Director of Communications

Part 5
Hālau Aomaluhiamauloa
House of Enlightenment & Peace

PROMOTING PEACE THROUGHOUT THE WORLD

Hālau Aomaluhiamauloa
House of Enlightenment and Peace

It is my view that LOVE is moving (and will continue to move) the Kingdom of Hawai'i forward; and when the Kingdom becomes fully restored, Aloha will spread all over the earth. Mother Earth is just waiting for this to happen. She is wishing to move from where we are, into this amazing new world, one that is full of ALOHA.

King Edmund Keli'i Silva, Jr. speaks about the Peace Center:

We shall be a non-aligned nation. We shall promote peace and create a Peace Center here in these islands for the Nations of the World to come talk story openly about taking care of their nations through peaceful solutions that are in Harmony with the spirit of aloha and the lands they live on.[66]

It is my sincere belief that King Keli'i Silva, Jr. deeply understands that the way of the new world, will be the "Kingdom Path" (the Path of Aloha), and he understands everything there is to understand about Aloha. He is here now, to help us (and the world) make this long awaited transformation.

A LETTER TO SECRETARY-GENERAL OF THE UNITED NATIONS, BAN KI-MOON - THE FUTURE IS CLEAR

Below are some excerpts from a letter to UN Secretary Ban Ki-moon about the future Peace Center:

The Kingdom of Hawai'i does not have the definitive solution to resolve the conflicts and hostilities that abound on our planet. I do, however, offer proposals that I believe are worthy of your attention.

In a vision, I saw the creation of a 'True' Peace Center, that stands firmly for "light, respect and love for all creation," built here in the Hawaiian Islands.

In that vision, the Hālau Aomaluhiamauloa – House of Enlightenment and Peace – united all nations to stand in solidarity as one voice and one people to protect the earth, land to sea, from unprecedented destruction that would change the landscape of our planet forevermore and, collaterally, destroy nations and the human-family...

While the tools of manipulation vary from one region to another, the pattern is the same. Ancient conflicts are kept alive to be used to stimulate hatred and anger. Clouded minds are then directed into attacking those painted as "the enemy." We cannot allow this manipulation to succeed.

I am sure you will agree that the time has come to put an end to these interminable conflicts that constantly threaten the peace and security of the Human Family. The Kingdom of Hawai'i has ancient knowledge that can bring about a change that will heal the hearts of its nation as well as, its lands and seas. The Kingdom is a non-aligned nation with no agenda internationally other than peace. The Kingdom invites the nations of the world to come to Hawai'i to explore the pathways to peaceful resolution of conflicts, starting with the conflict in the Middle East.

The Kingdom also invites all nations to embrace a season of peace. In ancient Hawai'i, each year brought the season of Makahiki. In this three month period, the law prohibited any war.

During that season, everyone came together, from whatever rank or position, to feast on the fruits of the Earth and engage in physical competitions, similar to the Olympics. The season of peace honored the Hawaiian God Lono, whose charge was to feed the people, and who represents the Earth.

There are messengers of peace in practically all the religions on Earth. We must come together to honor and implement those messages. **As a first step in the peace process, the Kingdom proposes that the nations of the world adopt and expand the Hawaiian Makahiki concept by declaring a year of peace in which all acts of violence, whether in the form of war or sectarianism, are forbidden.** *During that year, delegations can come to Hawai'i and/or Hawaiian conflict resolution specialists will come to regions in conflict, to share the blessings of ho'oponopono.*

His Majesty Edmund K. Silva, Jr.
Nou Ke Akua Ke Aupuni O Hawai'i

October 28, 2015

To: Secretary-General Ban Ki-moon
United Nations
760 United Nations Plaza
New York, New York 10017

Info: President Barack Obama
The White House
1600 Pennsylvania Avenue NW
Washington, D.C. 20500

Subject: Hālau Aomaluhiamauloa – House of Enlightenment and Peace

Aloha mai e Secretary General,

I am writing to you because I believe that the future bearing down upon us is becoming clear. We can see the chaos of war pushing Humanity towards an Armageddon abyss and climate chaos beginning to cause the collapse of civilization in various parts of the world. Those of us who are objective enough to look reality in the eye know that alternative pathways are desperately needed.

I am writing to offer such alternatives and to urge you to put the full force of your position behind these proposals by distributing this letter to the nations of the world for their consideration.

The Kingdom of Hawai'i does not have the definitive solution to resolve the conflicts and hostilities that abound on our planet. I do, however, offer proposals that I believe are worthy of your attention.

In a vision, I saw the creation of a 'True' Peace Center, that stands firmly for "light, respect and love for all creation," built here in the Hawaiian Islands. In that vision, the Hālau Aomaluhiamauloa – House of Enlightenment and Peace – united all nations to stand in solidarity as one voice and one people to protect the earth, land to sea, from unprecedented destruction that would change the landscape of our planet forevermore and, collaterally, destroy nations and the human-family.

Ka Pu'uhonua O Na Wahi Pana O Hawai'i Nei
kingdomofhawaii.info
hmkingdomofhawaii@gmail.com

http://en.wikipedia.org/wiki/List_of_bilateral_treaties_signed_by_the_Kingdom_of_Hawaii

The United Nations Charter provides the rest of the authority to do it." (*An autonomous independent sovereign nation-state contemplated under Article 1 of the 1933 Montevideo Convention on Rights and Duties of States requiring the state as a person of international law possessing the four qualifications of (a) a permanent population, (b) a defined territory, c) government; and (d) capacity to enter into relations with the other states.*)

Whereas, it is my sincerest goal to build Hālau Aomaluhiamauloa here in Hawai'i, until that center is established, we can still have meaningful talks about 'World Peace' either at the United Nations or here in Hawai'i. If here in Hawai'i, I will, with the aid of the Federal Government of the United States, arrange for this meeting to take place at the Convention Center on the Island of Oahu. Conflict re-solutionists will be gathered from throughout Hawai'i Nei to bring solutions to protect this planet and the Human Family.

Current events:

"China is not afraid of fighting a war against the United States in the South China Sea, a state-run newspaper with links to the Communist party has claimed. Twenty-four hours after Washington challenged Beijing's territorial claims in the region by deploying a warship to waters around the disputed Spratly archipelago, the notoriously nationalistic Global Times accused the Pentagon of provoking China.

"In [the] face of the US harassment, Beijing should deal with Washington tactfully and prepare for the worst," the newspaper argued in an editorial on Wednesday.

"This can convince the White House that China, despite its unwillingness, is not frightened to fight a war with the US in the region, and is determined to safeguard its national interests and dignity."

The People's Liberation Army Daily, China's leading military newspaper, used a front-page editorial to accuse the US of sowing chaos in countries such as Afghanistan and Iraq."

We know that the Kingdom of Hawai'i is a small nation still seeking to fully restore its membership in the community of nations. That does not mean that we cannot be creative in assisting the Human Family in seeking solutions to the challenges we all face.

For example, in the conflict just noted generated by competing claims to islands in strategic places, we could suggest a model for resolving that conflict. The restored Kingdom of Hawai'i is prepared to offer a peaceful solution. Through agreement with the other nations of the world, the Kingdom will establish the Kingdom Protectorate.

The Protectorate will take possession of all such islands under the following rules:

-- No facilities will be built on the islands to support military uses.

Ka Pu'uhonua O Na Wahi Pana O Hawai'i Nei
Nou Ke Akua Ke Aupuni O Hawai'i
kingdomofhawaii.info

http://en.wikipedia.org/wiki/List_of_bilateral_treaties_signed_by_the_Kingdom_of_Hawaii

The United Nations Charter provides the rest of the authority to do it." *An autonomous independent sovereign nation-state contemplated under Article 1 of the 1933 Montevideo Convention on Rights and Duties of States requiring the state as a person of international law possessing the four qualifications of (a) a permanent population, (b) a defined territory, c) government; and (d) capacity to enter into relations with the other states.*

-- If uninhabited, the conflict islands will be left in their natural state.

-- If inhabited, the Kingdom, and other cooperating nations, will assist the island population in becoming self sufficient and sustainable.

-- The surrounding fishing grounds will become sanctuaries to ensure replenishment of the rapidly dwindling fish populations worldwide. Only local populations on inhabited islands will be permitted to fish in those sanctuaries. The boundaries of such zones would be a matter of international agreement or default back to the normal territorial waters and exclusive economic zone methods of delimiting territory for sovereign nations.

-- Under sea deposits of oil and natural gas within the territory of an island nation will be placed in permanent reserve to avoid their contribution to climate chaos

-- If inhabited, the islanders can choose to remain a Protectorate with local self-government. That option is similar to the self-governing territory associated with a sovereign nation as envisioned in the United Nations Charter addressing non-self-governing territories.

-- If inhabited, the islanders can choose to become an independent nation with the agreement that they will be non-aligned. The nations of the world will agree not to pursue alliances with such nations and not to interfere in the internal affairs of such nations.

-- All islands within the Kingdom Protectorate will be subject to international inspection to assure all nations that the islands are remaining either demilitarized and/or refraining from militarization.

Is this proposal realistic? However you answer that question, I respectfully suggest that the proposal presents an alternative, unique approach to removing the threat posed by the islands in conflict. I also suggest that just such creative thinking is needed to change the current trajectory of history.

The Middle East is another flash point where the fuel is in place that could ignite and produce a worst case scenario for the Human future.

Ka Pu'uhonua O Na Wahi Pana O Hawai'i Nei
Nou Ke Akua Ke Aupuni O Hawai'i
kingdomofhawaii.info

http://en.wikipedia.org/wiki/List_of_bilateral_treaties_signed_by_the_Kingdom_of_Hawaii

The United Nations Charter provides the rest of the authority to do it." *An autonomous independent sovereign nation-state contemplated under Article 1 of the 1933 Montevideo Convention on Rights and Duties of States requiring the state as a person of international law possessing the four qualifications of (a) a permanent population, (b) a defined territory, c) government; and (d) capacity to enter into relations with the other states.*

Every bullet that is fired, every bomb that is dropped, and every religious site that is desecrated – all contribute towards creating an all out conflict, which the Human species would be fortunate to survive. Those who would divide the Human Family and foment a catastrophic war are attempting to take control of our history and send it down a dark road.

Here again, the Kingdom can serve as a neutral party to help resolve these conflicts. As a non-aligned nation, we do not judge any of the parties. The history of brutality, sectarian violence, imperial interference, and other contributors to the conflict can only be resolved when those in conflict are provided an opportunity to consider peace.

While the tools of manipulation vary from one region to another, the pattern is the same. Ancient conflicts are kept alive to be used to stimulate hatred and anger. Clouded minds are then directed into attacking those painted as "the enemy." We cannot allow this manipulation to succeed.

I am sure you will agree that the time has come to put an end to these interminable conflicts that constantly threaten the peace and security of the Human Family. The Kingdom of Hawai'i has ancient knowledge that can bring about a change that will heal the hearts of its nation as well as, its lands and seas. The Kingdom is a non-aligned nation with no agenda internationally other than peace. The Kingdom invites the nations of the world to come to Hawai'i to explore the pathways to peaceful resolution of conflicts, starting with the conflict in the Middle East.

The Kingdom also invites all nations to embrace a season of peace. In ancient Hawai'i, each year brought the season of Makahiki. In this three month period, the law prohibited any war.
During that season, everyone came together, from whatever rank or position, to feast on the fruits of the Earth and engage in physical competitions, similar to the Olympics. The season of peace honored the Hawaiian God Lono, whose charge was to feed the people, and who represents the Earth.

There are messengers of peace in practically all the religions on Earth. We must come together to honor and implement those messages. As a first step in the peace process, the Kingdom proposes that the nations of the world adopt and expand the Hawaiian Makahiki concept by declaring a year of peace in which all acts of violence, whether in the form of war or sectarianism, are forbidden. During that year, delegations can come to Hawai'i and/or Hawaiian conflict resolution specialists will come to regions in conflict, to share the blessings of ho'oponopono.

Ka Pu'uhonua O Na Wahi Pana O Hawai'i Nei
Nou Ke Akua Ke Aupuni O Hawai'i
kingdomofhawaii.info

http://en.wikipedia.org/wiki/List_of_bilateral_treaties_signed_by_the_Kingdom_of_Hawaii

The United Nations Charter provides the rest of the authority to do it." *An autonomous independent sovereign nation-state contemplated under Article 1 of the 1933 Montevideo Convention on Rights and Duties of States requiring the state as a person of international law possessing the four qualifications of (a) a permanent population, (b) a defined territory, c) government; and (d) capacity to enter into relations with the other states.*

Ho'oponopono is a technique of conflict resolution developed in Hawai'i over thousands of years. The essence of the ho'oponopono process is that the parties experiencing division agree to have a ho'oponopono practitioner resolve their conflict. That agreement has four steps: (1) All parties to the conflict agree that they will accept the resolution of the conflict developed through the ho'oponopono process. (2) All parties to the conflict come to the table and express their views on the nature of the conflict and their suggested resolution. (3) Based on all the presentations by the parties, the ho'oponopono practitioner pronounces the resolution of the conflict. (4) All the parties agree that the conflict will never be spoken of again.

The Kingdom offers this same process to the international community. As a non-aligned nation having no agenda other than peace, the Kingdom can pronounce resolutions to the conflicts that are not biased toward one party of another.

The agreement by the parties to abide by whatever resolution the ho'oponopono practitioner pronounces alleviates pressure on the conflicting parties to satisfy the demands of every faction within their own party. The more conflicts are resolved, the less fuel there is for new conflicts to arise. Those countries, organizations, or other entities that violate the ho'oponopono resolution or otherwise pursue conflict during the year of peace will reveal themselves to the rest of the world as purveyors of death. The international community can remove their support systems and isolate their infection.

The Kingdom believes that the Human Family can bridge from a house divided against itself to a renewed union as one family. In the Kingdom view, there are only two real issues: peace and reconciliation within the Human Family and peace and reconciliation between the Human Family and the rest of the Natural World.

The Kingdom stands ready to assist the rest of the family in achieving those goals. For those nations willing to embrace the year of peace and participate in resolving existing conflicts, I ask that you communicate that willingness to me.

I look forward to hearing from you and the governments throughout this planet. The time is now, that we must fix the mess of the generations of the past so that the generations succeeding us can have the blessings of living in a world filled with peace and respect for all of life and the human-family.

Ka Pu'uhonua O Na Wahi Pana O Hawai'i Nei
Nou Ke Akua Ke Aupuni O Hawai'i
kingdomofhawaii.info

http://en.wikipedia.org/wiki/List_of_bilateral_treaties_signed_by_the_Kingdom_of_Hawaii

The United Nations Charter provides the rest of the authority to do it." *An autonomous independent sovereign nation-state contemplated under Article 1 of the 1933 Montevideo Convention on Rights and Duties of States requiring the state as a person of international law possessing the four qualifications of (a) a permanent population, (b) a defined territory, c) government; and (d) capacity to enter into relations with the other states.*

Woodrow Wilson once said: "You are not here merely to make a living. You are here in order to enable the world to live more amply, with greater vision, with a finer spirit of hope and achievement. You are here to enrich the world, and you impoverish yourself if you forget the errand."

Please send any response you have to this message to my Ali'i Mana'o Nui (Chief Advocate) Lanny Sinkin: *lanny.sinkin@KingdomofHawaii.info*.

Respectfully yours,

Edmund K. Silva Jr.

Edmund K. Silva, Jr.
Ali'i Nui Mō'ī

cc: Na Kupuna Council O Hawai'i Nei ame Moku
Ali'i Mana'o Nui Lanny Sinkin
Minister of Foreign Affairs

Ka Pu'uhonua O Na Wahi Pana O Hawai'i Nei
Nou Ke Akua Ke Aupuni O Hawai'i
kingdomofhawaii.info

http://en.wikipedia.org/wiki/List_of_bilateral_treaties_signed_by_the_Kingdom_of_Hawaii

The United Nations Charter provides the rest of the authority to do it." *An autonomous independent sovereign nation-state contemplated under Article 1 of the 1933 Montevideo Convention on Rights and Duties of States requiring the state as a person of international law possessing the four qualifications of (a) a permanent population, (b) a defined territory, c) government; and (d) capacity to enter into relations with the other states.*

Part 6
Queen Lili'uokalani's Last Words

PICTURES OF THE ANNEXATION CEREMONY

I'm sure you would agree that a picture is worth a thousand words. Imagine the gut-wrenching sadness that permeated the islands on the day the Hawaiian flag was lowered, and replaced by the American Flag (called to this day, "the false flag"). This event took place on August 12, 1898, at the Iolani Palace.

Queen Liliuokalani, Princess Kaiulani, Prince David Kawananakoa in Washington Place in mourning on the day the flag of Hawaii was lowered for the last time after the Annexation of Hawaii to the United States.

QUEEN LILI'UOKALANI'S POWERFUL REMINDER "GOD IS NOT MOCKED"

Hawaii's Story by Queen Lili'uokalani

Below is a very powerful reminder at the end of Queen Lili'uokalani's book in regards to the future of the Kingdom of Hawai'i: [53]

> *"...be not deceived, **God is not mocked** ... and He will keep His promise, and will listen to the voices of His Hawaiian children lamenting for their homes."*

From the last chapter of "Hawaii's Story" [bold text added]:

Here, at least for the present, I rest my pen. During my stay in the capital, I suppose I must have met, by name and by card, at least five thousand callers. From most of these, by word, by grasp of hand, or at least by expression of countenance, I have received a sympathy and encouragement of which I cannot write fully.

Let it be understood that I have not failed to notice it, and to be not only flattered by its universality, but further very grateful that I have had the opportunity to know the real American people, quite distinct from those who have assumed this honored name when it suited their selfish ends.

But for the Hawaiian people, for the forty thousand of my own race and blood, descendants of those who welcomed the devoted and pious missionaries of seventy years ago, – for them has this mission of mine accomplished anything?

Oh, honest Americans, as Christians hear me for my down-trodden people! Their form of government is as dear to them as yours is precious to you. Quite as warmly as you love your country, so they love theirs.

*With all your goodly possessions, covering a territory so immense that there yet remain parts unexplored, possessing islands that, although near at hand, had to be neutral ground in time of war, do not covet the little vineyard of Naboth's, so far from your shores, lest the punishment of Ahab fall upon you, if not in your day, in that of your children, for "**be not deceived, God is not mocked.**"*

The people to whom your fathers told of the living God, and taught to call "Father," and whom the sons now seek to despoil and destroy, are crying aloud to Him in their time of trouble; and He will keep His promise, and will listen to the voices of His Hawaiian children lamenting for their homes.

It is for them that I would give the last drop of my blood; it is for them that I would spend, nay, am spending, everything belonging to me. Will it be in vain? It is for the American people and their representatives in Congress to answer these questions. As they deal with me and my people, kindly, generously, and justly, so may the Great Ruler of all nations deal with the grand and glorious nation of the United States of America.

Part 7
Current Issues

THE ALOHA AINA PROJECT

Executive Summary of the Aloha Aina Project

As it turns out, the *Aloha Aina Project* is not only a blue print for a revitalized, sustainable Hawaiian nation; it is a blueprint for ALL nations for sustainability. People all over the world are realizing how essential it is to leave the path of decay and destruction of our planet and return to the "husbandry" of the planet.

Excerpted from the Executive Summary of the Aloha Aina Project:[54]

> *The Hawaiian term, "Aloha Aina" literally means, "love of the land". In its deeper sense, Aloha Aina means love of the people, family (past, present and future), the community, nature, the environment, and all that physically and spiritually comprise the islands we call, Hawai'i.*
>
> *Hawaiian traditional values reflect Aloha Aina, incorporating the ancient Hawaiian practice of utilizing the talents and skills of everyone in the community, all working responsibly together in harmony, with a commitment for the present, and a heart for future generations.*

We believe that the time-honored traditional approach of shared vision, shared responsibility and industriousness also holds the key to a vibrant, modern society. It is upon this love for Hawai'i and its people that the Aloha Aina Project is built...

Ali'i Mana'o Nui Lanny Sinkin summarizes the *Aloha Aina Project* as follows:

Healing ecological wounds, reducing Human contributions to climate instability, transitioning to a fully organic agricultural system, establishing health and wellness centers and public health outreach programs, building affordable housing and providing a foundation of stability for the homeless, encouraging the development of new technologies that contribute to sustainability, transforming the educational system to train young people to think creatively about resolving the challenges we face as a species, and offering peace-making services to nations experiencing conflicts, are all part of the Aloha Aina Project.

Mission

Rebuild a Prosperous Society

The mission of the Aloha Aina Project is to facilitate the building of the people of Hawai'i into a vibrant, healthy and prosperous society, by using a comprehensive approach to raise and improve the overall quality of life in the Hawaiian Islands.

Problem

The Risk of Societal Collapse in Hawai'i

Despite outward appearances, Hawai'i is at risk of experiencing a devastating societal collapse due to serious flaws inherent in the systems, structures, programs and policies that currently prevail in Hawai'i. Conditions have greatly worsened over the last decade. The recent global fuel crisis and current economic meltdown are serving to underscore the urgency to implement immediate measures to save Hawai'i from collapse and chaos.

Solution

Self Reliance

- Aloha Aina Project believes the solution to the problem of dependency is — self-reliance.

- Aloha Aina Project believes the best way for Hawai'i to mitigate the harm that would follow from being cut off from the lifeline of imported goods, is to stop being so dependent on imported goods; to become essentially self-reliant.

- Aloha Aina Project believes that Hawai'i's health problems must be addressed and resolved, and that a large part of that solution is through a healthy diet and healthy lifestyles.

- Aloha Aina Project believes that Hawai'i's housing and high cost-of-living crisis is a reflection of a dysfunctional economic system that must be resolved.

- Aloha Aina Project believes the best way to provide Hawai'i's people with a bright and meaningful future is for Hawai'i to become inherently self-reliant. Not only would this put us out of danger, but the process of achieving self-reliance would serve to build a much stronger, more productive and caring community.

Primary Objective

The primary objectives of Aloha Aina Project are to extricate Hawai'i from its current vulnerable state of abject economic slavery (dependence on imported food, fuel, commodities, etc.), and to transform Hawai'i into a self-reliant, thriving, productive, prosperous, safe and vibrant island community.

Ali'i Mana'o Nui Lanny Sinkin Adds his View on the Aloha Aina Project

The Aloha Aina Project is a divinely inspired document that the King has brought forward as a vision of restoration. He knew what Hawai'i had been like before contact – it was a self-reliant island civilization with a political system that was designed for sustainability and a high state of health. Their medicinal system had been developed over thousands of years and was one that the Europeans didn't understand at all.

The Aloha Aina Project will restore things that are beneficial [to the Hawaiian culture] - like the food, the economic system, the social structures and especially the establishment of a Peace Center, which will focus on conflict resolution techniques known as Ho'oponopono --- and act as a non-aligned nation with services as an alternative to the United Nations.[69]

NATION WITHIN A NATION

The False Narrative:
Hiding the Truth about "Nation within a Nation"

Below is an excerpt from *The False Narrative*,[55] by King Keli'i Silva, Jr. and Ali'i Mana'o Nui Lanny Sinkin:

The seizure of the Queen was part of a systematic attack on all aspects of Hawaiian civilization that had been going on for years. Banning the hula, insisting on English only in the schools, outlawing ancestor worship, and other attacks on the foundations of Hawaiian civilization combined with the diseases brought by the foreigners to commit attempted genocide of the Hawaiian people and destruction of their civilization.

Despite the systematic attack, the Hawaiian civilization survived. That survival meant that the Hawaiian claims to their sovereignty and their lands also survived.

That miracle of resiliency is a matter of great discomfort for the United States. The failed attempt to legally annex Hawai'i, the phony statehood plebiscite, the legally ineffective Admissions Act, and all the other actions based on the corrupt foundation of the original crimes failed to extinguish the Kingdom or the Kingdom's legitimate claims to sovereignty and jurisdiction over Kingdom lands.

Today more modern techniques are being employed in an effort to complete the process of extinguishing the Kingdom.

The techniques for manipulating populations through the use of propaganda have been used for centuries. In recent times, Joseph Goebbels, Reich Minister of Propaganda in Nazi Germany, and Leni Riefenstahl, propaganda filmmaker in Nazi Germany, brought propaganda techniques to new heights of effectiveness.

Today, those techniques are being further refined to include manipulation of new communications channels, such as the Internet. The National Security State apparatus within the United States government (USNSS) is very busy pursuing such techniques.

One technique of the USNSS is creating a false narrative. The target population is to be manipulated into believing something other than the truth and into acting on that belief unaware that the belief is false. Such a false narrative can take over the conversation in such a way that the truth is submerged – not destroyed, just shoved out of the conversation. An excellent discussion of this technique is found here:

http://www.commondreams.org/views/2015/09/28/power-false-narrative

See also: http://tinyurl.com/nbypy66

There is a false narrative that is attempting to submerge the truth about the Kingdom of Hawai'i. In that false narrative, people of original Hawaiian ancestry are an "indigenous people," whose future should be addressed through laws, institutions, and programs that address indigenous rights.

King Keli'i Silva Jr. Discusses His View of "Nation within a Nation"

Here is an excerpt from one of his letters to President Obama, "International Court of Justice":[56]

> *Like any nation upon the earth, there will be challenges and adversities that will come up. What separates us from the rest of the world is our spirit of 'Aloha'. Aloha has taught us that as Kanaka Maoli, we have a bond of love that will never break and a love that will never be lost. When we exchange Ha (breath), shake hands, or hug each other, we see no wrongs, therefore, there is no sin. All we see is forgiveness and love for each other. This is the Hawaiian way that was in the beginning and is now.*
>
> *I issued "The Right to Self Determination" on June 23, 2003. You can review this document in the Independence Documents section of the Kingdom website. http://kingdomofhawaii.info/documents/.*
>
> *This document pronounced the reestablishment of the Kingdom of Hawai'i as an independent nation. From that day forward, the reality of the Kingdom's political existence began to shift towards independence. We have seen the effort by those who would extinguish the Kingdom and replace it with the equivalent of a Native American reservation for "Native Hawaiians." That effort failed.*

We have seen the United States Departments of Interior and Justice send representatives to the islands to ask what form of subservience would be acceptable. That effort also failed, as hundreds of people appeared at the hearings to reclaim their nation and invite the occupying power to go home.

More and more, the discussion shifted away from the bankrupt idea of nation-within-a-nation to restoration of the nation.

For the past twelve years, I have worked diligently to build our nation. I provided a vision and plan for the restored nation. I exposed the corruption of the governmental agencies, organizations, and individuals acting on behalf of the occupying power. I have stood with the practitioners of the traditional faith as they emerged from suppression to reclaim their right to practice.

The record of my actions can be seen in the documents posted on the Kingdom website at www.KingdomofHawaii.info.

I commend all those standing for what are right, particularly the young people waking up to the reality of our occupied nation. Resistance with Aloha is the path to liberation.

Onipa`a (Be) steadfast. This was the motto of Queen Liliuokalani who was overthrown by the Americans in 1893. Since 1993, the centennial commemoration of that event, Onipa`a has become a rallying cry for Hawaiians seeking redress and sovereignty.

The Kingdom is Purposely Excluded from "Nation within a Nation" Dialogue

Ali'i Mana'o Nui Lanny Sinkin sent the following email to the Kingdom's Email List explaining why the Kingdom is a necessary party in the *Na'i Aupuni* litigation, and why the litigation should be dismissed because the Kingdom is absent:

> The United States Department of Interior, the State of Hawai'i, the Office of Hawaiian Affairs, the Akamai Foundation, and the Na'i Aupuni Foundation are all cooperating in an effort the extinguish the Kingdom through the Na'i Aupuni process and the Department of Interior Proposed Rule. See the recent email with the subject "The False Narrative."
>
> A group of individuals have filed suit challenging the Na'i Aupuni process as racially discriminatory or otherwise defective. None of these individuals claim to represent the Kingdom.
>
> Yet the Kingdom has a significant interest in this litigation. The formation of the Native Hawaiian Government Entity will make completing the restoration of the Kingdom more difficult and change the relationship of a significant part of the Kingdom descendants with the United States. As the Department of Interior comments on the Proposed Rule state:
>
> "The government-to-government relationship with the Native Hawaiian Governing Entity would have very different characteristics from the government-to-government relationship that formerly existed with the Kingdom of Hawaii."

There is a rule in law that says a court has jurisdiction over a matter only if all the parties having an interest in the matter are before the court. If there is a "necessary" and "indispensable" party and that party is not and cannot be made a part of the litigation, the case must be dismissed.

The Kingdom is absent from the Na' Aupuni litigation. The Kingdom has interests in the litigation that are not represented. The Kingdom is a necessary and indispensable party. The King, as a sovereign, has not and will not subject the Kingdom to the jurisdiction of the United States Federal court. Under those circumstances, the case must be dismissed.

The Kingdom has filed a Notice of Absence of Necessary and Indispensable Party in the Na'i Aupuni case. We will update the network on any responses from the Court to that filing.

Pearl Means Warns the Hawaiian People about Settling for "Nation within a Nation"

Pearl Daniel-Means, of the Navajo Nation, had this to say about the heartbreaking consequences of the First Nations Peoples of America, when they acquiesced under duress into "Nation within a Nation" status: [36]

Should the United States Government attempt to negotiate a "Nation within a Nation" status with the Kingdom of Hawai'i, take note of what has happened to the First Nations Peoples of America. Quasi-sovereignty is what the First Nations of America have. Self-rule under federal supervision is not sovereignty.

When you stand on your legal lawful rights, it is irresponsible to compromise your rightful position. The moment The Kingdom of Hawai'i begins negotiating their rights they will have immediately lost those rights. Politics is the art of compromise, where true Leadership is based on principles.

That spark of light the American Indian Movement lit in the 1970's is dim and almost gone. We now look to you, our Hawaiian relatives to unite and ignite that light, and move this Independence Movement forward. Your position is legal and lawful and your time is now.

We stand with you in solidarity as you make your next move it is a tremendous step forward for all of us in the indigenous world.

We no longer have time to be idle, when our homelands are being desecrated, our water our lifeline continually poisoned and our children being stolen. As we witness all things we hold sacred and holy continually under attack, I'm reminded of Russell's words, "Everyone should get angry at injustice. People who don't certainly aren't spiritual people.

King Keli'i Summarizes "Nation within a Nation"

King Keli'i addresses *Ka Lāhui* Hawai'i regarding Nation within a Nation: [57]

To consider becoming a nation within a nation is playing with Fire; you would be giving up much more than your freedom; you would be inviting

Armageddon into your front yard. This is the reality that you are inviting into our homes by creating a nation with a nation government with the United States of America.

I am perplexed, even flabbergasted, that for a few pieces of Silver, the proponents of this obvious death to our nation is even being considered.

My question to you is this... is this the best choice for our people? Do we think so little of ourselves that we are willing to sell out our beloved inheritance and settle for less? Are you telling me and others that you don't love yourself enough to avoid living under the roof of stress, anger and despair?

Making the right decision is not difficult. At least for me it isn't. For you, it might take renewed determination to get to the truth. You must discern the truth about the motives of these less-than-honest Government Agents.

I ask you to strongly consider the following statement: OHA and the State of Hawai`i are trying to extinguish the Kingdom. They are attempting to divide the people of Hawaiian ancestry from the whole population in order to create a semi-independent government that will be dominated by the U.S Department of Interior. It is to their advantage to do this, not yours...

My closing thoughts ...

Why would we sign our own death warrants by creating a nation within a nation government? We have tremendous international support. Nations around the world are standing with us as we continue to restore our Nation. They stand with us because they know our cause is legal, lawful and just. The Kingdom of Hawai'i is your nation since time immemorial.

Just as the King warns us that division among us will ultimately lead to the demise of the Kingdom, 98 year old, Kupuna Aunty Ipo explains that division is already here: [75]

Aunty Ipo Addresses State-Controlled Division

These government agencies and groups are blocking us from the real battle in restoring our kingdom. Why are we playing into their hands like puppets on a string? There are plenty of issues to keep us all busy to be sure but that is what the no good forces wants us to do.

They are masters of deception. And, know how to weave a web of lies that sounds like the truth to deter us from the real issue of restoring our Kingdom.

They know how to push our buttons. Don't you think the Federal Agency of the United States as well as, The State of Hawai'i has studied us carefully? Sure they have and they have found our weaknesses. That's how they will beat us. As the old saying goes, divide and conquer. How much longer are you going to let the no good keep us down? What are you prepared to do?

MAUNA A WĀKEA

The Mauna a Wākea Protectors

One of the letters I wrote in support of the Mauna a Wākea Protectors, "We Protect Because We Love",[58] will introduce you to one of the many issues of Mauna a Wākea.

> **Mauna a Wākea was Akua's gift of Aloha to the Hawai'ian people eons ago.** As the Mauna a Wākea Protectors peacefully stand up for the mountain, they are peacefully expressing their love for the islands of Hawai'i, the culture of Hawai'i, the Hawai'ian religion and sacred places of Hawai'i --- they are, in truth, standing up for and expressing their love for the Kingdom of Hawai'i.
>
> Even though the Oppressors have attempted to swallow up and extinguish the Kingdom of Hawai'i, the Kingdom is alive! The Kingdom of Hawai'i is being fully restored through the leadership of Ali'i Nui Mo'i Edmund Keli'i Silva, Jr., and will one day retake her rightful place among the nations of the world. The Protector's love for the Mountain is igniting / re-energizing the Mountain, and in turn the Mountain is giving back. It is exhaling Aloha to all of Hawai'i and into the world.
>
> Whether they know it or not, the Protectors of Mauna a Wākea are "quickening the Spirit" of Hawai'i. King Keli'i Silva has lamented often via his writings, on the decapitated spirit of Hawai'i and her people. Hopefully though, this decapitated Spirit is reconnecting to the land and the people of the Hawaiian Nation...

The Sacred Mountain of Akua

It is my opinion that the relationship between "Akua" and "Aloha" is at the core of the Mauna a Wākea political issue. With that being said, I also believe that Mauna a Wākea (the sacred mountain of Akua) not only physically, but also spiritually, represents the essence of the Kingdom itself. It wasn't too long ago that a beautiful vison was cast about the Kingdom and the Mountain in a letter, "The King's Message to the Kingdom of Hawai'i". [62]

> *Much like a mountain surrounded in a mist, the Kingdom of Hawai`i exists. It is here among us. And though it has taken much longer than we would like for it to appear, it will eventually emerge from the mist, for all to see.*

The mist that I speak of is neither good nor bad, it just "is". But it is so real that it prevents access to the mountain. It allows you just enough of a view to see the outlines of a mountain, and allows your imagination to tell you what it might look like, feel like and smell like, while still beyond your reach.

I would equate this example of the misty mountain to loving someone so deeply, whom you do not have access to --- as she or he is behind the mist. They are so close to you, but untouchable. Oh the heartache and despair you have as you wait for the mist to depart and your beloved to come home to you.

This is what I know ... the mist will depart when the warmth and light of the sun appears and burns it away.

You are here, joined together with me because you love the land ... our beautiful, God-given ancestral lands. It was given to our ancestors in love, and it is our ancestors who lovingly cared for it all those long years ago. We are their children, tasked to keep the Kingdom of Hawai`i alive, and to work as hard as we can to restore it to its rightful place among the nations of the world.

Until now, I have freely addressed a variety of topics in this book, and done so with confidence; but writing about Mauna a Wākea without heavy reliance on the King's letters and Ali'i Mana'o Nui Lanny Sinkin's video appearance, would leave you with little understanding of the complicated issues that have been (and continue to be) dealt with.

Protecting the Protectors

King Keli'i is and Ali'i Mana'o Nui Lanny Sinkin are doing more than is even known to "protect the Protectors". They have been writing letters to President Obama, the Governor of Hawai'i, the State appointed political representatives for the issue, as well as pursuing legal means to resolve all the issues involved.

It is a known fact that "the Mauna Kea Protectors need protection" against the State of Hawai'i. King Keli'i has written many letters to Hawaii's Governor, David Ige, challenging him to make right (PONO) his erroneous actions. To date, the Governor has not been willing to address the issues with the King, and in fact, continued to sanction illegal arrests of the Protectors even after receiving the King's letters.

Although much was presented to the Governor in a recent letter by the King, "The Rule of Law Trumps the Resort to Violence", [61] I will only highlight the following paragraph as it is how I feel about the Governor and his "non-handling" of the situation:

> *You [Governor David Ige] are such a disappointment. The controversy that erupted around the proposed Thirty Meter Telescope on sacred Mauna a Wākea raised profound issues calling for the highest leadership response. Instead, you have resorted to official violence by continuing to pursue meaningless and illegal arrests of the Protectors of the Mountain.*

Previous letters to Governor Ige [63] can be found on the Kingdom of Hawai'i's Blog.

Mauna a Wākea Receives National Attention

Below, I've loosely transcribed a portion of a discussion between **Sean Stone of "Watching the Hawks" on RT and Lanny Sinkin**, which aired on 4-21-15. Be sure to watch the entire video, [64] as Lanny was given the opportunity to speak freely about the Kingdom's involvement with the Mauna a Wākea issues.

In regards to halting construction of the TMT telescope on Mauna a Wākea, Lanny Sinkin answers:

> *There are legal issues/lawsuits going on which are pending. The fundamental question is - who owns the land? And the right of spiritual practitioners of the ancient Hawaiian religion to be allowed freedom to practice their faith.*

Let me interrupt at this point and make a few observations:
It is significant to note that Lanny Sinkin spoke to a world-wide audience and presented the fundamental issue about the Mauna a Wākea controversy. This fundamental issue is:

Who has the right to make the decision about whether or not the construction of the telescope should be allowed? Is it the King or the Hawaiian State Governor?

Since you have been presented with the true facts and history of the illegal occupation of the Hawaiian Islands by the United States government, which is presently happening, you know the answer to this question...

KING EDMUND KELI'I SILVA, JR. SHOULD BE THE ONE MAKING DECISIONS ABOUT WHETHER OR NOT TMT HAS THE RIGHT TO DESECRATE THE SACRED MOUNTAIN OF AKUA. AND THE KING HAS STATED HIS DECISION ABOUT TMT NUMEROUS TIMES... "NO CONSTRUCTION WILL BE ALLOWED ON MAUNA A WĀKEA BY TMT".

Continuing now with the transcribed words of Lanny Sinkin...

There have been numerous efforts to stop the building of telescopes since 1970.

The protectors are not against science/astronomy - it is about protecting a sacred site – it's about a foreign government on a nation [that is not theirs] and it's time to de-occupy Hawaii.

There are other sites that telescopes can be built on, but no other sites can BE Hawai'i.

In 1893, a group of sugar growers rose up to overthrow the Queen, and the United States Minister to Hawaii, landed US marines to back up the sugar growers, and they seized the Queen and seized the Kingdom government, and that led to the overthrow of the Kingdom government.. The goal of that sugar grower movement was to annex Hawaii to the United States – to abolish the Kingdom altogether in order to avoid having to pay the tariffs on sugar that the United States had imposed on foreign sugar....

There has been a movement to restore the Hawaiian nation since 1893... it has been a 120 year political movement to reclaim the nation of Hawai'i.

At the time of the overthrow, Hawaii had treaties with major nations across the globe, and those treaties have never been relinquished by the Hawaiian people, the claims to their nation have never been relinquished, the claims to their lands have never been relinquished, they basically consider themselves to be an occupied nation trying to liberate itself and rejoin the community of nations.

Kingdom Litigation

Lastly, it is important to note that there have been legal cases filed on behalf of the Sacred Mountain of Mauna a Wākea by the Kingdom of Hawai'i. [27] Not only is the Kingdom working for a righteous outcome, the litigation is giving the Hawaiian State and Federal judicial system a chance to fulfill their mandate - which is to provide a fair trial, and allowing truth, justice and righteousness to prevail on the Mauna a Wākea issues. "The jury is still out". We shall find out in the near future if they are institutions of righteousness, or institutions of State and Federal self-interest.

UNTIL THE KINGDOM OF HAWAI'I IS TOTALLY INDEPENDENT FROM THE UNITED STATES GOVERNMENT... THERE WILL BE NO REST

Reaffirmation of Independence

I would like to conclude this book with a brilliant letter [67] by King Keli'i addressed to "the United States of America, the United Nations, and all Nations throughout the Earth".

THE KING SPEAKS THE TRUTH ABOUT HAWAI'I'S PAST, PRESENT, AND FUTURE IN THE FOLLOWING LETTER.

I would respectfully ask that you read this letter carefully and completely – let it reverberate in the depth of your Soul. It is up to us to spread Hawai'i's truth to the ends of the earth...

Hawaiian Archipelago

His Majesty Edmund K. Silva, Jr.
Nou Ke Akua Ke Aupuni O Hawai'i

April 21, 2015

Secretary-General Ban Ki-moon
United Nations
760 United Nations Plaza
New York, New York 10017

United Nations Security Council
United Nations
760 United Nations Plaza
New York, New York 10017

Secretariat of the Permanent Forum on Indigenous Issues (SPFII)
United Nations
Room S-2954
New York, New York 10017

President Barack Obama
The White House
1600 Pennsylvania Avenue, NW
Washington, D.C. 20500

Chief Justice John Glover Roberts
Supreme Court of the United States
1 First Street, NE
Washington, D.C. 20543

Secretary Sally Jewell
United States Department of the Interior
1849 C Street, N.W.
Washington D.C. 20240

Ka Pu'uhonua O Na Wahi Pana O Hawai'i Nei
kingdomofhawaii.info

http://en.wikipedia.org/wiki/List_of_bilateral_treaties_signed_by_the_Kingdom_of_Hawaii

The United Nations Charter provides the rest of the authority to do it." (*An autonomous independent sovereign nation-state contemplated under Article 1 of the 1933 Montevideo Convention on Rights and Duties of States requiring the state as a person of international law possessing the four qualifications of (a) a permanent population, (b) a defined territory, c) government; and (d) capacity to enter into relations with the other states.)*

Secretary John Kerry
United States Department of State
Room 7207
2201 C Street, NW
Washington D.C. 20520

Commissioner John Koskinen
United States Internal Revenue Service
500 N. Capitol St. NW
Washington, D.C. 20221

Alt: Commissioner John Koskinen
Room 2413
1111 Constitution Avenue, NW
Washington, D.C. 20224

Attorney General Eric Holder
United States Department of Justice
950 Pennsylvania Avenue, NW
Washington, D.C. 20530-0001

Secretary Ash Carter
United States Department of Defense
1400 Defense Pentagon
Washington, D.C. 20301-1400

The Honorable Kevin McCarthy
United States House of Representatives
2421 Rayburn House Office Building
Washington, D.C. 20515-0523

The Honorable Nancy Pelosi
United States House of Representatives
233 Cannon House Office Building
Washington, D.C. 20515-0512

The Honorable Mitch McConnell
United States Senate
317 Russell Senate Office Building
Washington, D.C. 20510-1702

Ka Pu'uhonua O Na Wahi Pana O Hawai'i Nei
Nou Ke Akua Ke Aupuni O Hawai'i
kingdomofhawaii.info

http://en.wikipedia.org/wiki/List_of_bilateral_treaties_signed_by_the_Kingdom_of_Hawaii

The United Nations Charter provides the rest of the authority to do it." *An autonomous independent sovereign nation-state contemplated under Article 1 of the 1933 Montevideo Convention on Rights and Duties of States requiring the state as a person of international law possessing the four qualifications of (a) a permanent population, (b) a defined territory, c) government; and (d) capacity to enter into relations with the other states.*

The Honorable Harry Reid
United States Senate
522 Hart Senate Office Building
Washington, D.C. 20510-2803

Governor David Y. Ige
State of Hawai'i
Executive Chambers,
State Capitol
Honolulu, Hawai`i 96813

Chief Justice Mark Recktenwald
Hawai'i Supreme Court
Ali`iolani Hale
417 South King Street
Honolulu, Hawai`i 96813-2943

Attorney General Doug Chin
State of Hawai'i
Department of the Attorney General
425 Queen Street
Honolulu, Hawai'i 96813

Maria E. Zielinski
Director of Taxation
State of Hawai'i
Princess Ruth Keelikolani Building
830 Punchbowl Street
Honolulu, Hawai'i 96813-5094

Deanna Saco
Director of Finance
County of Hawai'i
25 Aupuni Street
Suite 2103
Hilo, Hawai'i 96720

Ka Pu'uhonua O Na Wahi Pana O Hawai'i Nei
Nou Ke Akua Ke Aupuni O Hawai'i
kingdomofhawaii.info

http://en.wikipedia.org/wiki/List_of_bilateral_treaties_signed_by_the_Kingdom_of_Hawaii

The United Nations Charter provides the rest of the authority to do it." *An autonomous independent sovereign nation-state contemplated under Article 1 of the 1933 Montevideo Convention on Rights and Duties of States requiring the state as a person of international law possessing the four qualifications of (a) a permanent population, (b) a defined territory, c) government; and (d) capacity to enter into relations with the other states.*

Sovereign Rights Declaration

To
The United States of America,
The United Nations
And all Nations throughout the Earth

We are a Sovereign Nation with an established Lawful Government.

Be it known that I, Edmund Keli'i Silva, Jr., King of the Kingdom of Hawai'i, hereby declare that the entire archipelago and surrounding seas of the archipelago belong to the Kingdom of Hawai'i; that all peoples throughout the world are served notice that Hawai'i is an independent, non-aligned, sovereign nation ordained and sanctified by 'Creator.'

That on October 22, 2003, the Constitution of the Kingdom of Hawai'i and by its ratifications, the restoration of the Kingdom was signed and sealed in Royal Chambers by Ali'i Nui Mō'i Edmund K. Silva, Jr. and ratified by members of the House of Nobles and families of royal ancestry.

That, on November 23, 2002, the Proclamation announcing the restoration of the Kingdom of Hawai'i was published.

That on June 21, 2003, the Declaration of Independence proclaiming the restored independence of the Kingdom of Hawai'i was promulgated.

And that on June 23, 2003, a copy of the Declaration was hand delivered to President George W. Bush, President of the United States, at the White House and subsequently to Kofi Annan, Secretary-General of the United Nations, at the United Nations Headquarters.

<u>Federal and State Taxes Will Not Be Paid To The Occupying Nation of The Federal Government of the United States and it's subordinate State – State of Hawai'i or subordinate subdivision – County of Hawai'i</u>

International/National Constructive Notice

As the Kingdom government is restored through me, the Federal Government of the United States and all subordinate governments of the United States, such as the State of Hawai'i and County of Hawai'i, have no jurisdiction over me or the sovereign Kingdom of Hawai'i.

Ka Pu'uhonua O Na Wahi Pana O Hawai'i Nei
Nou Ke Akua Ke Aupuni O Hawai'i
kingdomofhawaii.info

http://en.wikipedia.org/wiki/List_of_bilateral_treaties_signed_by_the_Kingdom_of_Hawaii

The United Nations Charter provides the rest of the authority to do it." *An autonomous independent sovereign nation-state contemplated under Article 1 of the 1933 Montevideo Convention on Rights and Duties of States requiring the state as a person of international law possessing the four qualifications of (a) a permanent population, (b) a defined territory, c) government; and (d) capacity to enter into relations with the other states.*

The joint resolution of Congress used by the United States to pretend to annex the Kingdom was legally ineffective. One nation cannot impose its laws on another nation nor change the political status of another nation through adoption of a resolution.

The United States is a foreign government occupying this Kingdom unlawfully. Our national government was overthrown by the United States under duress and threat of life and liberty to her Royal Majesty Queen Lili'uokalani. Historical records show that she yielded her throne only temporarily to prevent loss of American and Kanaka Maoli life and with full expectation that the United States would restore her to her throne.

The overthrow of the Kingdom government directly violated the United States law known as the Neutrality act.

The Neutrality Act

18 USC § 960 - Expedition against friendly nation

> Whoever, within the United States, knowingly begins or sets on foot or provides or prepares a means for or furnishes the money for, or takes part in, any military or naval expedition or enterprise to be carried on from thence against the territory or dominion of any foreign prince or state, or of any colony, district, or people with whom the United States is at peace, shall be fined under this title or imprisoned not more than three years, or both.

This law makes it a crime for a citizen of the United States to engage in any military or naval expedition against a nation at peace with the United States.

In 1893, the Kingdom of Hawai'i and the United States had treaties in effect pledging, among other things, friendship and peace. A treaty in 1826 addressed friendship, commerce, and navigation. A treaty in 1849 also affirmed friendship. A treaty in 1875 established reciprocity in trade. In 1893, the Kingdom and the United States were definitely at peace.

Unquestionably, the actions taken by the group that overthrew the Kingdom of Hawai'i government constituted military action. Those actions were supported by Marines landed in Honolulu Harbor. Marines are within the United States Department of the Navy. The Marines acted under orders from the United States Minister, who did not have authorization to commit an act of war against the Kingdom. The Minister acted as a co-conspirator in the overthrow. The overthrow of the Kingdom government was, therefore, both a military and a naval expedition conducted in violation of the Neutrality Act.

Ka Pu'uhonua O Na Wahi Pana O Hawai'i Nei
Nou Ke Akua Ke Aupuni O Hawai'i
kingdomofhawaii.info

http://en.wikipedia.org/wiki/List_of_bilateral_treaties_signed_by_the_Kingdom_of_Hawaii

The United Nations Charter provides the rest of the authority to do it." *An autonomous independent sovereign nation-state contemplated under Article 1 of the 1933 Montevideo Convention on Rights and Duties of States requiring the state as a person of international law possessing the four qualifications of (a) a permanent population, (b) a defined territory, c) government; and (d) capacity to enter into relations with the other states.*

The purpose of the overthrow was ultimately to have the Hawaiian Islands annexed to the United States. The United States Minister acted in support of that illegal goal.

The private citizens involved in the overthrow, including most of the leadership, were United States citizens. Their participation in the overthrow violated the Neutrality Act. Had the law been enforced, these citizens would have been prosecuted and imprisoned. The United States Minister would also have faced criminal prosecution.

Instead, those seeking to destroy the Kingdom and annex Hawai'i to the United States formed the Provisional Government and proceeded to take control of the Kingdom government and lands. The United States Minister immediately recognized the illegal government, thereby furthering the conspiracy.

We need go no further in the history to understand that the seizure of the Kingdom was an illegal act of war even pursuant to domestic United States law. For the United States to later accept the poison fruits of that crime is simply a perpetuation of the original crime. Each day, the continued occupation of Hawai'i by the United States is an act in furtherance of the original conspiracy to annex the Kingdom.

The United States maintained the pretense of Hawaiian independence as the Provisional Government became the Republic of Hawaii. When the Spanish-American War broke out, the United States avoided formally occupying the Kingdom, as it did lands belonging to Spain, such as Cuba and Puerto Rico, by passing a joint resolution of Congress to annex our nation. Everyone who studies that episode now understands that no treaty of annexation was ever ratified by the United States Senate and that no joint resolution by one nation can change the legal status of another. In other words, the annexation process was legally ineffective and the Kingdom still exists.

Since the false annexation, the United States engaged in an extraordinary military build up in the Hawaiian Islands. While the Kingdom gave permission for a limited United States military presence prior to the overthrow, the United States military has dramatically expanded its military presence without Kingdom permission. The heavy military presence means that our nation is now essentially occupied by the United States.

Neither the false annexation nor the unauthorized military expansion gives any legitimacy to the United State Federal Government or any of its subordinate governments.

The United States admitted as such when, in 1945, the United States entered Hawai'i on the United Nations list of non-self governing nations.

Ka Pu'uhonua O Na Wahi Pana O Hawai'i Nei
Nou Ke Akua Ke Aupuni O Hawai'i
kingdomofhawaii.info

http://en.wikipedia.org/wiki/List_of_bilateral_treaties_signed_by_the_Kingdom_of_Hawaii

The United Nations Charter provides the rest of the authority to do it." *An autonomous independent sovereign nation-state contemplated under Article 1 of the 1933 Montevideo Convention on Rights and Duties of States requiring the state as a person of international law possessing the four qualifications of (a) a permanent population, (b) a defined territory, c) government; and (d) capacity to enter into relations with the other states.*

The United States later tried to undo that listing by holding a statehood election that excluded restored independence as an option.

That the United Nations allowed the United States to remove our nation from that list is shameful.

Nor can the United States levy taxes on any funds coming to me or the Kingdom. Taxation constitutes the occupying power taking property belonging to citizens of the occupied territory and transferring ownership of that property to the occupying power. The United States and its subordinate governments instituted the taxation of Kingdom citizens without notice or an opportunity for hearing.

> Without the guaranty of 'due process' the right of private property cannot be said to exist, in the sense in which it is known to our laws. The principle, known to the common law before Magna Charta, was embodied in that Charter (2 Coke, Inst. 45, 50), and has been recognized since the Revolution as among the safest foundations of our institutions. Whatever else may be uncertain about the definition of the term 'due process of law,' all authorities agree that it inhibits the taking of one man's property and giving it to another, contrary to settled usages and modes of procedure, and without notice or an opportunity for a hearing.

Ochoa v. Hernandez y Morales, 230 U.S. 139, 161 (1913).

Taxes being paid to the occupying nation are not lawfully applicable to me, my subjects, citizens, nobles and royal Household. I further repeat that the Federal Government of the United States has No jurisdiction upon my Kingdom, me, members of the Royal Family, Citizens, subjects and nobles.

Therefore, I, Edmund Keli'i Silva, Jr. HRM as the rightful heir and ruler of the Hawaiian Archipelago and the Hawaiian Kingdom do hereby present and confirm my Sovereign Rights Declaration. This document supersedes any organizational claim of any Foreign Country or De Facto state's claims of jurisdiction. The common-law rights of my Kingdom according to the Compiled Laws of the Hawaiian Kingdom guarantee myself as the Sovereign Ruler. They are both superior and senior to any contrary claim of Mosaic Law, Roman Canon Law, Foreign statutes or foreign regulations.

All Economic resources pertaining to my Kingdom to include but not limited to Financial Funding, Agriculture, Technology, and all Natural and Human resources remain under the sole jurisdiction of my command and order. They are hereby declared free from United States taxes on income, payroll, property, sales, capital gains, dividends, imports, estates and gifts, as well as various fees i.e. foreign tax, duty or tariff.

Ka Pu'uhonua O Na Wahi Pana O Hawai'i Nei
Nou Ke Akua Ke Aupuni O Hawai'i
kingdomofhawaii.info

http://en.wikipedia.org/wiki/List_of_bilateral_treaties_signed_by_the_Kingdom_of_Hawaii

The United Nations Charter provides the rest of the authority to do it." *An autonomous independent sovereign nation-state contemplated under Article 1 of the 1933 Montevideo Convention on Rights and Duties of States requiring the state as a person of international law possessing the four qualifications of (a) a permanent population, (b) a defined territory, c) government; and (d) capacity to enter into relations with the other states.*

Historical Letter dated March 12, 1898 by United States Senator Donelson Caffrey (D- Louisiana):
"...The present [Republic] government of Hawaii, which undertakes to cede territory to the United States, has no title to the islands, for the reason that their title is derived from the revolution instigated and carried to consummation by the United States Minister, Mr. Stevens. The revolutionists are not the representatives of the wishes of the people of Hawaii, and can convey no title to the sovereignty of territory, the control of which they have usurped...."

Hawaii Annexation. 1895, 1898-1899 Donelson Caffery letters commenting on the quasi-protectorate policy of the United States and McEnery's support of the treaty to annex Hawaii as a territory, 5 letters, v. 2, p. 257-260, 269-270; v. 3, p. 98; v. 6, p. 156-160. Caffery's opposition to the annexation of Hawaii, v. 6, p. 147.

It Is Done,

Edmund K. Silva, Jr.
Ali'i Nui Mō'ī

   cc: Na Kupuna Council O Hawai'i Nei Ame Moku
          Ali'i Mana'o Nui Lanny Sinkin

Ka Pu'uhonua O Na Wahi Pana O Hawai'i Nei
Nou Ke Akua Ke Aupuni O Hawai'i
kingdomofhawaii.info

http://en.wikipedia.org/wiki/List_of_bilateral_treaties_signed_by_the_Kingdom_of_Hawaii

The United Nations Charter provides the rest of the authority to do it." *An autonomous independent sovereign nation-state contemplated under Article 1 of the 1933 Montevideo Convention on Rights and Duties of States requiring the state as a person of international law possessing the four qualifications of (a) a permanent population, (b) a defined territory, c) government; and (d) capacity to enter into relations with the other states.*

Part 8
Resolved Issues

THE KING'S IMPRISONMENT AND THE ROYAL KUPUNA EXCHANGE

Facts According to Ali'i Mana'o Nui Lanny Sinkin

In discussing these two subjects, it is best to rely on the words and viewpoint of Ali'i Mana'o Nui Lanny Sinkin. He offers a first-hand account of these two incidences - not only from his service to the King, but as a federal attorney who has worked to bring forth truth and justice on behalf of the Kingdom of Hawai'i for well over a decade.

The King's Imprisonment

Excerpted from "The Mana of Hawai'i is Rising" [68] by Lanny Sinkin:

> **"How did you meet Edmund K. Silva, Jr.? What brought you two together?"**
>
> *When I asked Sam Kaluna where the King was in jail, he said Colorado. When I asked what he was charged with, Sam said "theft by deception." I told Sam that the Iran-Contra case was my only experience with criminal law, so I was not sure what that charge meant. I asked him how long the King was sentenced to be in prison. Sam said 24 years. I was astonished. I said: "Sam, murderers and rapists don't get 24 years." Sam said: "you're catching on." "Oh," I said, "it's political?" "Yes," he responded. He went on to*

explain that the King had been very active politically in the islands and was considered a serious problem by the political establishment because they were afraid he could mobilize people to restore the Kingdom. Sam also said that he had extensively reviewed the genealogies of a number of candidates and concluded that Keli'i was the one to be King.

I flew to Colorado to meet the King, taking with me a priest from the Temple of Lono, an ancient Hawaiian religion. We spent time with the King to hear his story and learn of his conditions. What I learned was that when Sam contacted him, he declined to accept the position, arguing that the government needed a King that was not in jail. Sam was very insistent, and Keli'i finally agreed. The priest gave him spiritual support and established an energetic link for him in the form of a rainbow bridge back to the islands.

Upon my return to the islands, I set about working on getting him released on parole. He had already been in prison for something like 12 years by that time. There is a whole story to be told about the efforts to secure his release that ultimately led to my turning the matter over to Spirit and his successful application to be released. He has now served out his parole time and is once again a free man.

"What convinced you that he was truly the King (namely, Ali'i Nui Mō'i)?"

When I examined the nature of the charges against him and heard his explanation of what had happened, it made sense to me that he was a political prisoner. The criminal charge was based on a speculative investor requesting the return of funds already invested. There was nothing criminal about what happened. Even a civil suit to recover the investment was unsupported. The facts suggested the presence of some other reason for the prosecution and imprisonment.

Subsequently, I discovered that there were covert operations being run against the King in prison. Those efforts sought to frustrate the King's efforts to reanimate international recognition for the Kingdom and secure the resources necessary to implement restoration of the Kingdom government. The elaborate nature of the covert operations, including the cooperation of the prison, as well as state and federal officials, demonstrated to me that, whatever I might think, the United States officials were convinced that he could succeed.

My extensive conversations with him during the time that he remained in prison only solidified my conviction that he was the one. While I am by no means knowledgeable about Hawaiian genealogies, I have enough knowledge to know that the King's genealogy would have been highly respected in the Kingdom and qualify him for the position.

While there are surely others that have a genealogy that would qualify them to fill the position, they have chosen not to step forward. Certainly none of them have offered the leadership that the King has provided, both in offering a vision and plan for the restored nation and in responding to the daily challenges faced by the Kingdom.

I was impressed with the support that 98 year old, Kupuna Aunty Ipo expressed for the King. She was able to look beyond the trumped up charges that prevailed against King Keli'i and see that he was a "political prisoner". Read Aunty Ipo's words...

> *There isn't any doubt in my mind that he was set up to look bad in the judgment of his people and the world because of who he is. Those that conspired against him tried hard to discredit him in the eyes of us all and temporarily succeeded , until now. I am the voice crying out from the wilderness asking you to hear me for I testify to you, that what I am saying is the whole raw truth".*
>
> *I have met him but once in my life. And, in that short time, I had chicken skin and felt the presence of Heaven upon him. I say these truths because I know without doubt he is the prophecy foretold over 200 years ago of he who would lead and restore our Hawai'i nei."*[75]

The Royal Kupuna Exchange

Below is the story about the *Royal Kupuna Exchange,* as told by Lanny Sinkin on a radio interview with Kauilapele on 10-24-14.[69] I transcribed his words and present the story below. In addition to the radio interview, Lanny Sinkin wrote a letter[70] about this issue, which you may wish to view.

> *Listen to this story as a lesson… what we're dealing with is people who have had their nation stolen from them 130 years ago and have been subject to all kinds of abuse –* **their [the Hawaiian people] religious system was taken away from them, their social system was taken away, their language was taken away for a while … their**

economic system of shared land ownership - all of the systems that created their civilization were either disrupted or destroyed by the missionaries and their descendants, *and that has badly damaged the people of Hawaii, [and these are the people] who we are now trying to rally to restore their nation.*

The effect of that kind of abuse is that people are very quick to judge - whether they're good, bad or indifferent, without taking the time to thoroughly explore what has really gone on.

The Story of the Royal Kupuna Exchange begins here...

A man came to some of the elders on the island of Hawai'i who said that he had access to a lot of gold and wanted to donate it to the restored kingdom. These elders had already drawn up documents and written the constitution to restore the kingdom, and they had selected Edmund K Silva, Jr. as the King.

This man suggested that they issue bonds that would be backed by this gold and use the proceeds of the bonds to restore the nation – to set up the government, do the programs - all these things, etc.

Thinking this was a great idea, they created the Royal Kupuna Exchange, which supposedly was offering bonds backed by gold. Because they had selected Keli'i as the King, they included him on the website – in other words, they mentioned him as King on the website.

I [Lanny] called him (the King was still in prison at the time) and asked if he knew anything about the Royal Kupuna Exchange - he said that he did not. The King said he never gave permission to put his name on that website and he didn't know anything about it.

So I [Lanny] contacted the webmaster and requested that the King's name be taken off the website or otherwise, the website itself should be taken down.

As it turned out, the man who said he had the gold was a con artist, he conned the elders so that he could take the money and run; but he was exposed, and that's when I [Lanny] insisted the website be taken down because it was based on a fraud.

Meanwhile the authorities had taken enforcement action against the website, but the damage was done ... the King's name was on the website.

I [Lanny] scoured the internet trying to tell these various website owners the facts. Even where some were taken down, the websites are cached (stored in the ethers) on the internet so you can still find some of those pages ... and some website owners won't take it down because they like having the King discredited by a false story because they are opposed to the kingdom's restoration.

Part 9
The Man, as King

TRUTH COMES IN TWO FACES

When a vision comes from the thunder beings of the West, it comes with terror like a thunder storm; but when the storm of vision has passed, the world is greener and happier; for wherever the truth of vision comes upon the world, it is like a rain. The world, you see, is happier after the terror of the storm...

You have noticed that **truth comes into this world with two faces.** *One is sad with suffering, and the other laughs; but it is the same face, laughing or weeping... as lightning illuminates the dark, for it is the power of lightning that heyokas have.*

Black Elk (Oglala Lakota Medicine/Holy Man)

It is important to note here, that I have written thus far about Edmund Keli'i Silva, Jr., in his role as King. But although a King, he is also one of us - living on earth at this time, to do what all of us are here to do, which is to love one another and to do good. Keli'i Silva, Jr. is a father, a grandfather, a son, a brother, an uncle. He is a friend to many people all over the world. Simply put, he is a man, who just happens to also be a King.

I cannot end this book until I have shared one last fact about King Keli'i. Few people understand how greatly he has suffered for his beliefs and willingness to restore the Kingdom of Hawai'i.

Before I write about the suffering that King Keli'i has experienced, I must first remind myself that it was my Lord, Jesus Christ, who suffered for simply being a Wayshower of the love and light of His Heavenly Father. He suffered much for His message; a message lasting to this day, which speaks of Godly love, peace and good will towards one another, to ourselves, and to all of earthly life. It is because of this message of the resurrected Christ, that King Keli'i (as well as myself), am able to embrace, and do our part to move the Kingdom forward.

Black Elk reminds us... "truth is made known with two faces"; in other words, the truth and authenticity of a man, is by his life experiences of duality; joy and sorrow, good and evil, lightness and darkness. Truth is then understood, (not only by the man himself, but also by those whose lives he touches), from the way he chooses to incorporate all of his experiences into his character.

King Keli'i has suffered more than most men for his belief in, and work towards, Kingdom restoration. His suffering includes years of false imprisonment and time away from his beloved family, the loss of loved ones, being ignored as he walks among his fellow men and women and communicates to world leaders; yet, he continues on his path with humility and great love for the Hawaiian people and the sacred islands of Hawai'i.

It is my strong belief that his words are not ignored in the realm of the invisible (the realm of the spirit). His words are powerful and life-changing, because every day there are mighty breakthroughs that miraculously move the Kingdom forward.

King Keli'i stands firm in his strong conviction of truth and righteousness, and he expresses his deep desire to honor his past commitments to family, friends and supporters. He never gives up. He prays to God for the freedom of the Hawaiian people from the chains of economic slavery that were long ago foisted upon the land and the people. He will never give up on his sacred mission to restore the Kingdom of Hawai'i to her rightful place among the nations of the world, nor will he leave the life-path he has agreed to walk upon.

TO KNOW HIM, IS TO UNDERSTAND THE SPIRIT OF ALOHA; TO UNDERSTAND A LEADER WHO IS STEADFAST AND STRONG AND COMMITTED TO LOVE, RATHER THAN POLITICAL AGENDA. KING KELI'I WILL BRING FREEDOM TO THE HAWAIIAN PEOPLE AND THE SACRED LANDS OF HIS ANCESTORS, WHO ARE THE ALI'I OF YESTERYEAR.

King Keli'i has required a steady spirit and strong conviction in his sacred path (kuleana) in order to have weathered the false imprisonment, slander, mockery and disrespect shown towards his person and the Kingdom. Even so, his many years of suffering has molded his character, and made him the formidable Warrior that he is today.

From the depths of darkness which was thrust upon him, he rose up, and leads the fight to this day, to restore the Kingdom, empowered by heavenly light of Akua. And despite the "heavy hand" which has constantly been raised against him, by people who do not wish to see the Kingdom restored, the King has prevailed, and made the case for Hawaiian Sovereignty and Independence to people and leaders all over the world.

He will continue to so, and although his work is "invisible" to most of the people now dwelling on the islands, he is actively working on behalf of these very people and their ancestral (and adopted) lands – the islands of Hawai'i Nei. What follows are a few of the King's recent letters to national leaders, which demonstrates his never-ending vigilance to protect the islands, the people of Hawai'i, as well as our beloved planet.

His Majesty Edmund K. Silva, Jr.
Nou Ke Akua Ke Aupuni O Hawai'i

January 26, 2016

To: His Excellency Kim Jong Un
Chairman
Chosun Communist Party
Kumsoosan, Miam-dong, Daesung district
Pyongyang, Democratic People's Republic of Korea (DPRK)

President Barack Hussein Obama II
1600 Pennsylvania Avenue, NW
Washington, D.C. 20500

His Excellency Xi Jinping
President of the People's Republic of China
premier@mail.gov.cn

President Vladimir Putin
Russian Federation http://eng.letters.kremlin.ru/
4, Staraya Square, Moscow, 103132 – Russia.

President Park Geun-hye
Cheongwadae, Sejong-ro No. 1, Jongno-gu, Seoul 110-820, Republic of South Korea
E-mail: webmaster@president.go.kr , foreign@president.go.kr

Prime Minister Mr. Kim Hwang-sik
Central Government Complex, 55 Sejong-no, Jongno-gu
Seoul, Korea 110-760

Ka Pu'uhonua O Na Wahi Pana O Hawai'i Nei
kingdomofhawaii.info
hmkingdomofhawaii@gmail.com

http://en.wikipedia.org/wiki/List_of_bilateral_treaties_signed_by_the_Kingdom_of_Hawaii

The United Nations Charter provides the rest of the authority to do it." (*An autonomous independent sovereign nation-state contemplated under Article 1 of the 1933 Montevideo Convention on Rights and Duties of States requiring the state as a person of international law possessing the four qualifications of (a) a permanent population, (b) a defined territory, c) government; and (d) capacity to enter into relations with the other states.*)

His Excellency Ban Ki Moon,
Secretary General of United Nations
United Nations Plaza
New York, New York 10017

Subject: Peace – Now More than Ever.

Aloha Oukou: H.E. Kim Jong Un, President Barack Hussein Obama II, His Excellency Xi Jinping, President Vladimir Putin, President Park Geun-hye, Prime Minister Mr. Kim Hwang-sik and H.E. Ban Ki Moon,

E pili mau na pomaika`i ia `oe — May blessings ever be with you.

As an ancient Chinese adage goes, "The greatest ideal is to create a world truly shared by all." Peace, development, equity, justice, democracy and freedom are common values of all mankind and these are achievable through understanding and respecting each other's Nations, culture, tradition and spiritual beliefs, and through treating each other with respect and dignity.

Humbly, I am deeply disturbed at the escalating tension between the People's Republic of North Korea and the United States. There is talk of missiles capable of reaching from North Korea to Hawai'i and of missile defense systems being deployed in Hawai'i to counter that threat.

While I have taken many steps to restore the Kingdom of Hawai'i as a fully independent member of the community of nations, I am still not in a position to prevent the lands and waters of the Kingdom from being used by foreign powers for their purposes. That does not mean that I approve of such actions.

To North Korea, I state unequivocally that the Kingdom of Hawai'i has no issues with you. We desire nothing more than peaceful relations and joint efforts to improve the quality of life for all the Human Family and to restore vibrant health to the ecosystems that the Human Family has so badly damaged.

Ka Pu'uhonua O Na Wahi Pana O Hawai'i Nei
Nou Ke Akua Ke Aupuni O Hawai'i
kingdomofhawaii.info
hmkingdomofhawaii@gmail.com

http://en.wikipedia.org/wiki/List_of_bilateral_treaties_signed_by_the_Kingdom_of_Hawaii

The United Nations Charter provides the rest of the authority to do it." *An autonomous independent sovereign nation-state contemplated under Article 1 of the 1933 Montevideo Convention on Rights and Duties of States requiring the state as a person of international law possessing the four qualifications of (a) a permanent population, (b) a defined territory, c) government; and (d) capacity to enter into relations with the other states.*

If you have issues with the United States, those issues are between your two nations and do not involve my Kingdom directly. If we can be of any assistance in facilitating peaceful exchanges to resolve those issues, we stand ready to perform that service.

To the extent those issues threaten my people with being targeted for military action; I call upon both parties to acknowledge the existence of our Kingdom as a non-aligned nation and to respect our neutrality.

From North Korea, we request a pledge not to attack the Kingdom of Hawai'i.

From the United States, we call for cancellation of the plan to place missile defense systems on the Island of Kaua'i.

There is surely enough conflict in the world without generating more. The Human Family seems determined to drag itself into the abyss. The Kingdom stands for peace and reconciliation within the Human Family and for peace and reconciliation between the Human Family and the rest of the Natural World. We call upon all nations of the Earth to embrace these two goals.

In Closing:

I am looking forward to ending conflicts throughout the world and it starts here with you not wanting to launch Nuclear Missiles at my Kingdom. It's okay to feel the need to express one's displeasures with your neighbors as long as you do so for the right reasons, at the right time, for the right cause, and with honor, compassion and wisdom.

To possibly launch Nuclear Missiles at my Islands would be wrong. Innocent people would suffer for the sake of those not willing to sit down and iron out their difficulties. Leadership is about working in harmony solving issues with positive results. Not threatening another nation without provocation. Although we are a non-aligned nation, I will stand in solidarity to support the peaceful policies of any nation and to condemn those that seek to impose their will on others. Every nation has the sovereign right to live in peace. Therefore, let peace be the only discussion and not threats. Threats serve no divine purpose.

Ka Pu'uhonua O Na Wahi Pana O Hawai'i Nei
Nou Ke Akua Ke Aupuni O Hawai'i
kingdomofhawaii.info
hmkingdomofhawaii@gmail.com

http://en.wikipedia.org/wiki/List_of_bilateral_treaties_signed_by_the_Kingdom_of_Hawaii

The United Nations Charter provides the rest of the authority to do it." *An autonomous independent sovereign nation-state contemplated under Article 1 of the 1933 Montevideo Convention on Rights and Duties of States requiring the state as a person of international law possessing the four qualifications of (a) a permanent population, (b) a defined territory, c) government; and (d) capacity to enter into relations with the other states.*

Why I wrote this letter should be obvious. I had no choice. Exercising my sacred duties to protect this Nation from attacks is absolute. Leaders who claim to be enlightened know there is no other way towards peace except the right way and that way is making peace within yourself, your nation, your neighbors and the nations of the world. I can assure you, once you do this, you will develop friends who will be most supportive of you and your noble ideas to serve your people and this planet we all share.

To reiterate, your issues, if any, are with those whom you feel have offended you and your Nation. The Kingdom of Hawai'i and its' people have done nothing to warrant any reprisals from your government towards mine.

We ARE the Kingdom of Hawai'i.

"In 1893, our Nation, the Kingdom of Hawai'i, was stolen. In 2004, I accepted the calling to be King of these Hawaiian Islands by Prime Minister Samuel Kaluna a descendant of the Original Members of the ancient Hawaiian House of Nobles. Therefore, in accepting this sacred duty the Kingdom is restored — I am the Direct Hereditary King of Hawai'i."

Declaration Signed October 21, 2004

Ua Mau ke Ea o ka 'Aina i ka Pono,

Edmund K. Silva, Jr.

Edmund K. Silva, Jr.
Ali'i Nui Mō'ī

cc: Na Kupuna Council O Hawai'i Nei ame Moku
        Ali'i Mana'o Nui Lanny Sinkin
        Chief Justice Kingdom of Hawai'i
        Minister of Foreign Affairs

Ka Pu'uhonua O Na Wahi Pana O Hawai'i Nei
Nou Ke Akua Ke Aupuni O Hawai'i
kingdomofhawaii.info
hmkingdomofhawaii@gmail.com

http://en.wikipedia.org/wiki/List_of_bilateral_treaties_signed_by_the_Kingdom_of_Hawaii

The United Nations Charter provides the rest of the authority to do it." *An autonomous independent sovereign nation-state contemplated under Article 1 of the 1933 Montevideo Convention on Rights and Duties of States requiring the state as a person of international law possessing the four qualifications of (a) a permanent population, (b) a defined territory, c) government; and (d) capacity to enter into relations with the other states.*

THE WHITE HOUSE

WASHINGTON

May 6, 2016

Mr. Edmund K. Silva, Jr.
Hilo, Hawaii

Dear Edmund:

Thank you for writing. The United States does not ignore what happens beyond our borders, and we are committed to promoting peace, security, and human rights throughout the world.

Through its provocative and destabilizing behavior, pursuit of weapons of mass destruction and their means of delivery, and systematic, widespread human rights abuses, North Korea has isolated and impoverished its people and intensified its threat to international peace and security—including that of the United States. Alongside our allies and partners around the world, we have condemned this behavior, enhanced efforts to deter and defend against threats, and strengthened the multilateral sanctions regime to demonstrate that there are consequences for North Korea's actions.

My Administration is determined to prevent North Korea from achieving its stated goals of advancing its nuclear program and gaining international acceptance as a nuclear weapons state while pursuing economic development. In addition to working with partners to fully enforce United Nations Security Council resolutions, I signed a new Executive Order to facilitate the implementation of additional sanctions of unprecedented breadth and strength, and to underscore our resolve to deter North Korea's destructive behavior. I am determined to stand by our country's ironclad commitment to defend treaty allies in the region.

We also share the international community's concern about human rights abuses in North Korea. The United Nations Commission of Inquiry has documented past and current abuses in painstaking detail, and we will continue working closely with our partners and allies to expose these actions and press North Korea to acknowledge and cease these serious violations.

North Korea has a choice: It can follow a path where it meets its obligations and enjoys greater security and prosperity, or it can stay on a course of confrontation and face more pressure and isolation. I remain open to opportunities for credible dialogue, but my Administration will not reward North Korea for undermining peace and stability or for defying the international community. We will continue to hold North Korea accountable for destabilizing and repressive actions, and we will sustain our unbreakable alliance with South Korea.

Thank you, again, for writing.

Sincerely,

Barack Obama

His Majesty Edmund K. Silva, Jr.
Nou Ke Akua Ke Aupuni O Hawai'i

July 7, 2016

President Vladimir Putin
Russian Federation 4
Staraya Square, Moscow, 103132 – Russia

Aloha President Putin:

This letter is not enjoyable to write. In the last communications we shared regarding sovereignty and self-determination, I became uniquely mindful that both you and I may have come from the same school of thought that leadership means providing careful judgement and consideration of our actions. That our actions can either further disrupt an already broken and fragmented world or take the sacred and positive position of healing the Natural world by spending National funds, human resources, and energy repairing and restoring our nations' ecosystems and mitigating the climate crisis now before us.

Finding and fighting for cures to homelessness, cancer, heart disease, diabetes and all types of illness and sicknesses of the mind and body, as well as, finding cures to heal, restore and repair our contaminated soil, polluted oceans, rivers and the hearts and minds of our people, is the greatest and most profound actions we as leaders can and must take. This is what in my opinion we should be investing our National resources into.

Spending a tremendous amount of National Funds to create and test yours or any other Nations Nuclear Missile only furthers the distrust and feeds into fear and self-destructive behavior we already see in the increase of terrorist attacks spreading around our world.

If indeed it is true that your proposed plan is to test your Nuclear Missile by firing the missile towards Hawaiian waters, this plan is unacceptable and irresponsible leadership.

Ka Pu'uhonua O Na Wahi Pana O Hawai'i Nei
kingdomofhawaii.info
hmkingdomofhawaii@gmail.com

http://en.wikipedia.org/wiki/List_of_bilateral_treaties_signed_by_the_Kingdom_of_Hawaii

The United Nations Charter provides the rest of the authority to do it." (*An autonomous independent sovereign nation-state contemplated under Article 1 of the 1933 Montevideo Convention on Rights and Duties of States requiring the state as a person of international law possessing the four qualifications of (a) a permanent population, (b) a defined territory, c) government; and (d) capacity to enter into relations with the other states.*)

See article dated July 1, 2016, that Pravda published regarding the launching of the Sarmat monster ICBM towards my Kingdom – Hawai'i. http://www.pravdareport.com/russia/kremlin/01-07-2016/134903-sarmat_missile-0/#

The article reports on the new missiles that the Russian Federation is developing to replace their current ICBMs and the testing program for the new missiles. That testing program is described as follows:

> In this case, the Russian military have to launch the new missile from the north to the area of the Hawaiian Islands. This is a complex, but a necessary test that Russia has to conduct, experts believe.

This action, regardless of the reasons behind it, is an act of aggression against my Kingdom. Otherwise, why would your military need to prove that the new missile can reach the Hawaiian Islands?

Your State Department or Minister of Foreign Affairs did not reach out to give us the respect we deserve by asking permission to test your Nuclear Missile in the direction of my Kingdom.

And were you to have asked permission, I would have respectfully said no.

On May 30, I raised similar objections with His Excellency Kim Jong Un, Chairman of the Chosun Communist Party in the Democratic People's Republic of Korea, to the missile testing by his nation aimed towards Hawai'i. I copied you with that letter and enclose another copy with this letter for your information. I also enclose the response to that letter I received from President Barack Obama.

Our reefs and sea life are being destroyed by man's need to continue to create large weaponry to destroy one another. The huge RIMPAC naval military exercise now happening in our waters brings that destruction to our shores. This I do not now nor will I ever agree to. As King, I am committed to peace and working in harmony with the Natural world and the Human Family.

Therefore, I strenuously object to this targeting of missiles in the vicinity of the Hawaiian Islands. While such targeting may be "sending a message" to the United States, the message is also received by the Kingdom of Hawai'i.

Ka Pu'uhonua O Na Wahi Pana O Hawai'i Nei
Nou Ke Akua Ke Aupuni O Hawai'i
kingdomofhawaii.info
hmkingdomofhawaii@gmail.com

http://en.wikipedia.org/wiki/List_of_bilateral_treaties_signed_by_the_Kingdom_of_Hawaii

The United Nations Charter provides the rest of the authority to do it." *An autonomous independent sovereign nation-state contemplated under Article 1 of the 1933 Montevideo Convention on Rights and Duties of States requiring the state as a person of international law possessing the four qualifications of (a) a permanent population, (b) a defined territory, c) government; and (d) capacity to enter into relations with the other states.*

As you know, our Kingdom is essentially an occupied country since the United States, in 1893, provided military support to a handful of sugar grower's intent on overthrowing the legitimate Kingdom government. The United States eventually claimed to annex the Hawaiian Archipelago. The overthrow constituted an act of war by the United States against a nation with whom the United States had a treaty of peace. The "annexation" took place pursuant to a joint resolution of the two houses of the United States Congress without the agreement of the Hawaiian people.

A movement to restore our nation's independence began the day that Queen Liliu'okalani was seized. I am part of that continuing effort. I have pursued restoration of the Kingdom Government for the past twelve years and documented our work at www.KingdomofHawaii.info.

Prior to the overthrow, the Kingdom participated in the international community as a recognized sovereign nation, choosing to remain a non-aligned nation devoted to peaceful relations among all nations. Our remerging nation embraces that same position of neutrality.

As you well know, and have spoken of quite recently, those who pursue a New World Order, based on assuming that order should embrace the agenda of the Project for a New American Century, have brought death and misery to many areas of the world.

http://speisa.com/modules/articles/index.php/item.508/putin-the-builders-of-the-new-world-order-have-failed.html?utm_campaign=shareaholic&utm_medium=facebook&utm_source=socialnetwork

Clearly the Kingdom is not a part of nor does it support in any way that effort. The Kingdom has been a victim and not a perpetrator. Based on these realities, I urge you to reorient your missile testing to avoid the Kingdom. As part of your support for transitioning from a uni-polar geopolitical landscape to a multi-polar landscape, you can announce the change in missile testing plans as a gesture of support for the liberation of the Hawaiian Kingdom.

As you are aware, it has been my intentions to sit down with you and discuss 'Treaty Agreements' between two Sovereign Nations: The Kingdom of Hawai'i and the Russian Federation.

I have been invited to make a presentation to a conference in Moscow sponsored by the Anti-Globalization Movement of Russia. Prior to or after the anti-globalization meeting, I would like to sit with you to discuss the future of my Kingdom, the Kingdom of Hawai'i. Specifically, I would like to discuss a possible 'Treaty' agreement between both our nations.

Ka Pu'uhonua O Na Wahi Pana O Hawai'i Nei
Nou Ke Akua Ke Aupuni O Hawai'i
kingdomofhawaii.info
hmkingdomofhawaii@gmail.com

http://en.wikipedia.org/wiki/List_of_bilateral_treaties_signed_by_the_Kingdom_of_Hawaii

The United Nations Charter provides the rest of the authority to do it." *An autonomous independent sovereign nation-state contemplated under Article 1 of the 1933 Montevideo Convention on Rights and Duties of States requiring the state as a person of international law possessing the four qualifications of (a) a permanent population, (b) a defined territory, c) government; and (d) capacity to enter into relations with the other states.*

We have made great progress in restoring the Kingdom Government and bringing the topic of that restoration into the public discussion. In a current legal proceeding in the United States, the Kingdom filed an objection to the proceeding because the Kingdom is not a party. I am enclosing a copy of that objection because that document will provide you with an overview of our current situation.

As part of my vision and plan for the Kingdom, we will build a Peace Center to offer a neutral meeting ground for those nations (and others) in conflict. We sincerely believe that the hour is upon us for Human civilization to prevent an ecological catastrophe and that the need to address this threat makes any further pursuit of war both obsolete and a distraction from the real challenge we face.

In closing: I shall end this letter by saying Onipa'a. (Be) steadfast.

Explanation: Take your stand and be steadfast in doing what is right no matter what others say. This was the motto of Queen Liliu'okalani, who was overthrown by the Americans in 1893. Since 1993, the centennial commemoration of that event, Onipa`a has become a rallying cry for Hawaiians seeking redress and Hawaiian sovereignty.

I look forward to a constructive and fruitful discussion at your earliest convenience.

Ua Mau ke Ea o ka 'Aina i ka Pono,

Edmund K. Silva, Jr.
Ali'i Nui Mō'i

cc: Na Kupuna Council O Hawai'i Nei ame Moku
Ali'i Mana'o Nui Lanny Sinkin
Chief Justice Kingdom of Hawai'i
Minister of Foreign Affairs

Ka Pu'uhonua O Na Wahi Pana O Hawai'i Nei
Nou Ke Akua Ke Aupuni O Hawai'i
kingdomofhawaii.info
hmkingdomofhawaii@gmail.com

http://en.wikipedia.org/wiki/List_of_bilateral_treaties_signed_by_the_Kingdom_of_Hawaii

The United Nations Charter provides the rest of the authority to do it." *An autonomous independent sovereign nation-state contemplated under Article 1 of the 1933 Montevideo Convention on Rights and Duties of States requiring the state as a person of international law possessing the four qualifications of (a) a permanent population, (b) a defined territory, c) government; and (d) capacity to enter into relations with the other states.*

Epilogue

WE CONTINUE ON A RIGHTEOUS PATH

It is Time!

I am now at the end of the story and realize that there is much of my own story interwoven within the telling of Hawai'i's story.

It is fitting that I came back to my hometown to write most of this book, and today, I am writing the end of the story at a place where my memories began. When I was a child, it was called, Woodrow Hill, and I'm sitting on the ground with a tree behind my back, overlooking the very spot where my dad took me to catch my first fish. Oh how proud I was of that little sunfish (perch), which I took home to show my mom.

White Rock Lake became my place of refuge, my place of adventure, my teacher of nature; it was the place I rode my horse and learned to distinguish the different bird songs and seasonal breezes. As I'm sitting here looking out, I am able to remember what it was about my life that led to such a passion in my heart for the Kingdom of Hawai'i. I will tell you now that I feel like I've come home. I am doing exactly what I was always meant to do – to work toward the reestablishment / restoration of the Kingdom of Hawai'i.

WHY ME, Alie James? Well, I definitely know why. When I was a young girl, I developed a very strong desire for truth, justice, fairness and righteousness – these feelings were planted deep within my heart. This happened because I lived through a few stressful years of name calling and bullying. This is one of the main reasons that I relate to the pain and injustice that the Hawaiian people have suffered, and why I understand the reason they are seeking sovereignty – they desire what I have always desired - truth, justice, fairness and righteousness for their nation.

But why is it that I turned my heart toward Hawai'i? There are countries all over the world that need the same things as the Kingdom of Hawai'i does. That's a fair question, and I will tell you why my heart is aligned with Hawai'i.

In the fall of 1985, I had an idea that my family and I should go to Hawai'i; it started out as a thought in my mind; it then became a verbal discussion, and finally it became a prayer. Two months later, right before Christmas, my family and I arrived in Hilo, Hawai'i, having secured employment that paid for our move.

Princess Ka'iulani

While in Hilo, I learned all about the history of Queen Lili'uokalani and the Crown Princess Ka'iulani. I developed a deep sorrow for them and their nation, even though at the time, I didn't understand that I was actually grieving for their entire Kingdom. But for them, I grieved and tried to understand why it happened.

Also while in Hawai'i, I was casually exposed to the Sovereignty movement; but it was in 2012 that I finally began to understand the reason for the movement, and the tragic events that befell their nation.

What happened was that one day, I was visiting a website that I frequented - Kauilapele's Blog, [74] and I came across a post that featured a letter by King Edmund Keli'i Silva, Jr. From that point on, I began to read the King's letters whenever they were posted on the blog. By nature, I am a researcher and **I realized early on that Edmund Keli'i Silva, Jr. was the one that Queen Lili'uokalani figuratively handed the mantle to**. I am not unique in this view, and I have referenced many people [32] in this book who have responded to King Keli'i in the same way as I have.

My feeling that he was the rightful heir became stronger over the last few years as I began to study every letter, proclamation and video of the King, as well as that of his Chief Advisor, Lanny Sinkin. Also, I frequented the Kingdom's website [17] and Blog. [46]

What I have just expressed to you is the reason for my Hawaiian connection, but even stronger than that, is my sincere belief that there is a paradigm shift taking place on our planet. I am a student of cyclical history and have known for about 20 years that sometime around 2012, we would begin to see a change in our world. (As an aside, when I was a young teen, it made no sense to me how the song, "Age of Aquarius" became a musical hit, but I now believe it was heralding the shift that we are now in – going from the Age of Pisces to the Age of Aquarius.)

Rather than become directly involved with world events and politics, I simply watch events unfold. What is significant to me, is watching the political power and influence shift from the west to east. All of this background information is important, because you will then understand this statement:

I believe the Kingdom of Hawai'i is at the center of it - the entire global shift - and because of this, the Kingdom of Hawai'i will retake her place as the heartbeat of our planet.

Those of us who have followed the writings of King Keli'i Silva throughout the years have come to understand his role as King, and Hawai'i's role as a non-aligned nation.

Please note, that I did not site letters or people, such as Mikahala Roy [33], Lanny Sinkin and Auntie Ipo, [75] without a good reason. These are leaders who have lived under the military occupation of the United States government and their proxy, the Hawaiian State government. Also, I featured the letter of Pearl Means, [36] which tells you what devastating effects have taken place because of the Navajo tribe (and the First Nations) compromising with the United States government on the issue of sovereignty. They are giving you first-hand information so that you can experience through their words, how it feels to desire, and work towards sovereignty.

So, you may be wondering ... how is it that I am qualified to write the story of Hawai'i Nei ... a story of such heartache, if I myself haven't felt Hawai'i's heartache? Again, this is a fair question.

My answer is that I am NOT qualified by birth or with a first-hand experience, but I am qualified to write this story because I have made myself a vessel. I have allowed myself to receive the story, and as a writer, the story has become mine.

Although I haven't felt the heartache of the Hawaiian people or felt the oppression perpetrated upon them, I do understand the truth of what happened; and most importantly, I understand from a spiritual point of view their loss.

My spirit has been guiding me throughout my lifetime to prepare for this story - the story of the Hawaiian nation's grievous loss, and now I am here, at this time, to write about it.

As a writer of non-fiction it is important to structure the story with facts, and that I have attempted to do. I've written a narrative that is sequenced in such a way as to make sense to people who have never heard the story, as well as make sense to those who have lived the story, but have not yet put all the pieces of the puzzle together.

Lastly it is written for those who have lived the story and understand it well – it stands as a record of yesterday's sorrow and today's hope. I have written a factual account of the events over the last 120 plus years, and done so with sincere passion.

In contrast, Hawaii, as the 50th State, has crafted a wonderful myth throughout the last century - a beautiful story of white sandy beaches, hula girls, luaus, tropical paradise; yet all along, hiding the truth of their ugly past and continued occupation of a friendly nation. My purpose in writing this story is to give you the information you need to form your own opinion about Hawaii the state, and Hawai'i the Kingdom.

As I said, we are going through a planetary change. One that will eventually move us away from war, elitism, imperialism, ill health, short lives, polluted land, water, air and food. It's a sea change and Hawai'i IS going to be at the forefront of the change, and that is because the devastating effects of her history, WILL BE MADE RIGHT, and also, the KINGDOM OF HAWAI'I WILL SHOW US A NEW WAY. (See the Aloha Aina Project). [50, 54]

It has been said – the meek shall inherit the earth. This will be the prevailing characteristic of the citizens and leaders of our planet in the future. Do not be confused. Meekness is a not weakness; meekness is strength.

Meekness is having a trusting, gentle spirit that seeks to love one another and provide stewardship of the planet. It is found in a people who rise up and do right - with strength of character, filled with the Spirit of Aloha. This is my idea of meekness.

The Kingdom of Hawai'i has a King – one who is leading us away from the old story of Hawai'i's past, and into the new story of Hawai'i's future.

Would you like to be at the forefront of this global change? I know I do, and I will one day return to Hawai'i and work alongside the leaders of the Kingdom government.

We, who have not yet made it back home to Hawai'i Nei, let us walk across a rainbow bridge – like the one that Ali'i Mana'o Nui Lanny Sinkin had made for his King, Keli'i Silva all those years ago. This rainbow bridge will bring us all home. As I often listen to Brother Iz (Israel Kamakawiwo'ole), it is no surprise that one my favorite songs is his version of "Somewhere Over the Rainbow".[74]

I am calling out to you – People of the Light.

Join in my efforts to help the King move the Kingdom forward. I am calling you in the Spirit of Aloha, as I have nothing to gain, except peace of mind that I am fulfilling my kuleana.

We are the ones who will contribute to the healing of the land; we are the ones who will make right the terrible wrongs done to the Hawaiian people. We will speak love and kindness to those who have suffered so much loss, and they will learn to love us and trust us once again.

Now I'll end with my personal story. I mentioned earlier that I was bullied during my childhood, and that is what ultimately led to my passionate desire for truth, justice, fairness and righteousness. During those years (and later throughout my life), I would cry out to God... Why am I so different? Why don't people understand me? The answer was always the same (at 12 years old, at 21 years old, at 30, 40, 50 years old and so on).

The answer ... "You have something very important to do - you are a like a pied piper". So, I would then ask – What is it that I'm supposed to do? Who am I leading, and where am I leading them to? In early 2000 I thought I understood what this meant.

I thought I was to speak to women about health and wellness and how to live their best life; so I wrote many health and wellness books. But for some reason, I could never muster the passion for the topic, even though I am passionate about my own health. A few years ago I finally discovered what I was to do, and where and who I was leading people to.

I was to lead "people of the light", and "people of love", back home to Hawai'i.... to the Kingdom of Hawai'i, and I was to point to the Nation's leader - a Warrior of Love and Light --- King Edmund Keli'i Silva, Jr., the Ali'i Nui Mō'i of Hawaii Nei. It is he, who is forging the *Path of Aloha* for us, and who I believe completely understands the needs of Hawai'i, as well as our planet. Hawai'i is the Kingdom of Love and Light – this is an aspect that is invisible to most, but not for much longer.

We, who love this King, love him unconditionally – and that is in response to the way he loves us. We are simply responding to the way he expresses his Aloha for the people and the land of Hawai'i.

There are people and leaders all over the world who have joined with us to restore the nation and to spread the King's message:37

> *"The Kingdom path is the Path of Aloha,*
>
> *A love for all creation, and a belief that we can create what we know in our hearts is the highest expression of who we are as a species.*
>
> *Come! Join us in creating and celebrating the new civilization."*

It is my fervent hope that this book will be a catalyst for the final decoupling of the Kingdom of Hawai'i from the United States. I know that I won't rest until this is accomplished and the Kingdom of Hawai'i emerges from "behind the mist", to take its rightful place among the nations as a non-aligned nation. Hopefully, as the truth is revealed to a new audience, the United States government will be compelled to do the right thing and provide restoration and restitution to the legitimate, restored Kingdom of Hawai'i, for the crimes committed against the nation of Hawai'i and her Queen, Lili'uokalani.

UNTIL THEN, IT IS UP TO THOSE OF US, WHO UNDERSTAND THE TRUE HISTORY OF THE KINGDOM OF HAWAI'I, TO SHARE WHAT REALLY HAPPENED IN 1893, AND WHAT IS CONTINUING TO HAPPEN - CONSPIRACY, INVASION, OVERTHROW & ILLEGAL OCCUPATION. IT IS ALSO UP TO US TO STEP UP AND HELP KING EDMUND KELI'I SILVA, JR., TO FULLY RESTORE THE KINGDOM OF HAWAI'I TO NATION STATUS.

Beautiful days are ahead in Hawai'i Nei.
Ku I Ka Mana!

For many of us, the things "of the Spirit" tend to be elusive – just beyond our reach. They are invisible to our eyes; yet, for those of us who wish to see, we will see, and those of us who wish to hear, will hear. These are the days we are in, when the invisible becomes visible. Not because the things we now see and hear have changed, but because we, as people, are changing.

Having come to the end now, I must say that it has been a complete joy to research and write on the subject of Hawai'i's dark past, and her light-filled future.

Knowing that we all wait with expectation for "the future" to arrive, we are left to live in "the present". While doing so, we have a man, standing in the gap – that man is King Edmund Keli'i Silva, Jr. He is a man, who is not only exposing the truth of Hawai'i's past and offering hope for Hawai'i's future; he is showing us how to live the *Path of Aloha*.

So now... we will watch as the mist dissipates.

Invisible, now Visible.

The King and the Kingdom.

Ku I Ka Mana Hawai'i Nei.

Po'o Huna 'Ano, Kumaka.
'O ke Ali'i Nui Mo'i a 'Ō Ke Aupuni ō Hawai'i.
Ku I Ka Mana Hawai'i Nei.

"Much like a mountain surrounded in a mist, the Kingdom of Hawai`i exists. It is here among us. And though it has taken much longer than we would like for it to appear, it will eventually emerge from the mist, for all to see...

This is what I know ... the mist will depart when the warmth and light of the sun appears and burns it away." [62]

                    King Edmund Keli'i Silva, Jr.

FREEDOM IS A GIFT

I am leaving you now with the inspiring words of the King of Hawai'i Nei, King Edmund Keli'i Silva, Jr.[71]

What makes us who we are -- is our allegiance to an idea that articulated our history of listening to the spiritual voice within aloha. Today we continue a never-ending journey to bridge these living and moving philosophical truths with the realities of our time.

For history tells us that while these inalienable rights may be self-evident and absolute, they've never been self-executing; that **while freedom is a gift from Heavenly Father, it must be safeguarded by His people here on Earth. We, as the human family, must come together to right the substantial wrongs, not just here in Hawai'i, but all over the world.**

Let us begin here and let our example resonate around the planet bringing the healing that is so desperately needed.

References

1. "The Kingdom Chant".
[https://www.youtube.com/watch?v=IqwZR-bjeEs]

2. "The Invisible King". 11-7-14
[https://kauilapele.wordpress.com/2014/11/07/the-invisible-king-a-letter-from-the-pen-of-alie-james/]

3. "Right to Self Determination". 5-14-13
[http://kingdomofhawaii.info/wp-content/uploads/2015/01/kingdomofhawaii.info_Right-to-Self-Determination.pdf]

4. "Reaffirmation of Independence". 4-21-15
[https://kingdomofhawaiiinfo.wordpress.com/2015/04/22/alii-nui-moi-edmund-k-silva-jr-4-21-15-taxes-proclamation/]

5. The "Apology Resolution".
[https://en.wikisource.org/wiki/Public_Law_103-150]

6. The Legalities of "whereas" statements. [http://legal-dictionary.thefreedictionary.com/Whereas].

7. The James Blount Report.
[http://libweb.hawaii.edu/digicoll/annexation/blount.html]

8. The Newlands Joint Resolution.
[https://en.wikipedia.org/wiki/Newlands_Resolution]

9. The Organic Act. [https://en.wikipedia.org/wiki/Organic_Act]

10. Queen Lili'uokalani's "Official Protest Against Annexation".
[https://books.google.com/books?id=QrTCvcy0sE4C&pg=PA354&dq=%22I+Liliuokalani,+by+the+Grace+of+God&hl=en&sa=X&ved=0CCUQ6AEwAWoVChMIwsq-lIb9xwIVw4I-

Ch0yEA_A#v=onepage&q=%22I%20Liliuokalani%2C%20by%20the%20Grace%20of%20God&f=false]

11. "The Ku'e Anti-Annexation Petition of 1897" video. [https://www.youtube.com/watch?v=RhRHLGZJkQA]

12. "President Cleveland's Message to Congress 1893". [http://www.hawaii-nation.org/cleveland.html]

13. "List of Bilateral Treaties Signed by the Kingdom of Hawaii" on Wikipedia. [https://en.wikipedia.org/w/index.php?title=List_of_bilateral_treaties_signed_by_the_Kingdom_of_Hawaii&oldid=558240308]

14. "Professor Francis A. Boyle Testimony - Restoration of Hawaiian Independence". [http://www.hawaii-nation.org/boyleall.html]

15. Hawaii's Story by Hawaii's Queen. 1898. Chapter LV.

16. "Kingdom of Hawaii" on Wikipedia. [https://en.wikipedia.org/wiki/Kingdom_of_Hawaii]

17. "Kingdom of Hawai'i Website". [http://kingdomofhawaii.info/]

18. "The Apology Resolution". [http://kingdomofhawaii.info/wp-content/uploads/2015/01/kingdomofhawaii.info_docs_apology_resolution.pdf]

19. Hawaii's Story by Hawaii's Queen. 1898. p 43.

20. "Unification – Royal Proclamation". 5-9-13 [http://kingdomofhawaii.info/wp-content/uploads/2015/01/kingdomofhawaii.info_docs_Unification.pdf]

21. "House of Kamehamehanui Ai'luau (Kamehameha nui 'Ai Luau)". [http://www.royalark.net/Hawaii/maui.htm]

22. "Royal House of Pi'ilani". [http://www.ulukau.org/elib/cgi-bin/library?e=d-0somr-000Sec--11haw-50-20-frameset-book--1-010escapewin&a=d&d=D0.4&toc=0]

23. "House of Maui-loa". [http://www.mauiculture.net/mookuauhau/]

24. "House of Hawai'i-loa". [http://www2.hawaii.edu/~dennisk/voyaging_chiefs/hawaiiloa.html]

25. "House of Kumuhonua". [http://www.sacred-texts.com/pac/hm/hm23.htm]

26. "Law and Morality". 7-6-15 [https://kauilapele.wordpress.com/2015/07/18/kingdom-of-hawaii-blog-alii-nui-moi-edmund-k-silva-jr-7-16-15-kings-letter-to-governor-ige-law-and-morality/]

27. "Kingdom Litigation for Mauna a Wākea". [http://kingdomofhawaii.info/mauna-a-wakea-sacred-mountain-litigation/]

28. "The Sacredness of Mauna Kea Explained". [http://welivemana.com/articles/sacredness-mauna-kea-explained]

29. "Definition of Ni'au pi'o - Hawai'i's Sacred Royal Child Blood Line". 1865. [https://books.google.com/books?id=jRRKAAAAcAAJ&pg=PA417&lpg=PA417&dq=ni%27au+meaning&source=bl&ots=dpyLHbmT9G&sig=pWTSHhkx7maafV-H_BH1iTYWv4I&hl=en&sa=X&ved=0CFUQ6AEwB2oVChMIhrSY9_TJxwIVzDk-Ch1JkA3O#v=onepage&q=ni%27au%20meaning&f=false]

30. "Keōpūolani - Queen Consort of Hawaii " on Wikipedia. [https://en.wikipedia.org/wiki/Ke%C5%8Dp%C5%ABolani]

31. "King Kekaulike, King of Maui, father of Kamehameha Nui 'Ai Lau'au". [http://www.mauiculture.net/mookuauhau/]

32. "Letters of Support -The Mana of All Hawai'i is Rising Facebook Page".
[https://www.facebook.com/thekingdomofhawaii/app_128953167177144]

33. "Mikahala Roy – E Nana i ke Kumu i Ke Ali'i Nui Mo'i". 7-8-15 [https://kauilapele.wordpress.com/2015/07/16/kingdom-of-hawaii-blog-lamaku-mikahala-roy-7-8-15-e-nana-i-ke-kumu-i-ke-alii-nui-moi-o-ka-aina-and-mauna-kea-conveyance/]

34. "Russell Means - American Indian Activist".
[http://www.economist.com/news/obituary/21565906-russell-means-american-indian-activist-died-october-22nd-aged-72-russell-means]

35. "Where White Men Fear To Tread: The Autobiography of Russell Means" by Russell Means and Marvin J. Wolf. 1995
[http://www.amazon.com/gp/product/B00WL8J12W/ref=dp-kindle-redirect?ie=UTF8&btkr=1]

36. "Pearl Daniel - Solidarity in support for the King and the Kingdom of Hawai'i". 7-11-15 [http://kingdomofhawaii.info/wp-content/uploads/2015/08/Pearl_Means-Official-DocumentProtected.pdf]

37. "Come Sit" on the King's Speech Video.
[https://youtu.be/sE_lwFzepTQ?t=8m11s]

38. "Peaceful End". 3-15-15
[https://kauilapele.wordpress.com/2015/03/06/from-kingdom-of-hawaii-blog-alii-nui-moi-edmund-k-silva-jr-3-5-15-kings-message-to-the-world-peaceful-end/]

39. "Coming Together in Peace". 4-3-15
[http://kingdomofhawaii.info/wp-content/uploads/2015/04/Coming-Together-In-Peace-3-4315.pdf]

40. "Philosopher King" on Wikipedia.
[https://en.wikipedia.org/w/index.php?title=Philosopher_king&oldid=674748333]

41. "Ship of State" on Wikipedia.
[https://en.wikipedia.org/w/index.php?title=Ship_of_State&oldid=641346178]

42. "The Paradox of the Philosopher King".
[http://www.loyno.edu/~folse/Philking.html]

43. "Mana of All Hawai'i is Rising" Facebook Page.
[https://www.facebook.com/thekingdomofhawaii]

44. "Marcus Aurelius" on Wikipedia.
[https://en.wikipedia.org/wiki/Marcus_Aurelius]

45. "Montevideo Convention" on Wikipedia.
[https://en.wikipedia.org/w/index.php?title=Montevideo_Convention&oldid=670662891]

46. "Kingdom of Hawai'i Blog".
[https://kingdomofhawaiiinfo.wordpress.com/]

47. "Moving Forward". 8-14-15
[https://kauilapele.wordpress.com/2015/08/18/kingdom-of-hawaii-blog-8-14-15-alii-nui-moi-edmund-k-silva-jr-kings-letter-to-governor-ige-moving-forward/]

48. "Rebuilding the Government of the Hawaiian Kingdom".
[http://kingdomofhawaii.info/wp-content/uploads/2015/01/kingdomofhawaii.info_docs_gov_narrative.pdf]

49. "The King's Speech" video.
[https://www.youtube.com/watch?v=sE_lwFzepTQ]

50. "The Aloha Aina Project". [http://kingdomofhawaii.info/wp-content/uploads/2015/01/kingdomofhawaii.info_docs_aloha_aina_narrative.pdf]

51. "Establishing Our Government". 8-12-15
[https://kingdomofhawaiiinfo.wordpress.com/2015/08/13/alii-nui-moi-edmund-k-silva-jr-8-12-15-establishing-our-government/]

52. "Ka Hae Hawaii - The Sacred Meaning of the Flag of the Kingdom of Hawai'i" . [http://kingdomofhawaii.info/wp-content/uploads/2015/05/Sacred-Meaning-of-Our-Nations-FlagApproved.pdf]

53. "Hawaii's Story by Queen Lili'uokalani". 1898
[http://digital.library.upenn.edu/women/liliuokalani/hawaii/hawaii.html]

54. "The Aloha Aina Executive Summary". 8-24-15
[https://aliejamesllc.files.wordpress.com/2015/04/executive-summary-aloha-aina-project-foundation.pdf]

55. "The False Narrative". 10-2-15
[http://kingdomofhawaii.info/wp-content/uploads/2015/10/The-False-Narrative.pdf]

56. "International Court of Justice". 4-7-15
[http://kingdomofhawaii.info/wp-content/uploads/2015/04/1-First-Capital-Kamakahonupdf-2.pdf]

57. "Letter to Ka Lahui Hawai'i regarding Nation within a Nation". 9-23-15
[https://kingdomofhawaiiinfo.wordpress.com/2015/09/24/alii-nui-moi-edmund-k-silva-jr-9-23-15-kings-letter-to-ka-lahui-hawaii-re-nation-in-nation/] Ka Lāhui Hawai'i

58. "We Protect Because We Love". 8-1-15
[https://aliejamesllc.files.wordpress.com/2015/04/mauna-kea-protectors_protecting-with-love.pdf]

59. "Royal Biography of Edmund Keli'i Silva, Jr.". 10-7-15
[https://aliejamesllc.files.wordpress.com/2015/04/royal-bio-eks-2015.pdf]

60. "Kingdom of Hawai'i Independence". 5-14-13
[http://kingdomofhawaii.info/wp-content/uploads/2015/01/kingdomofhawaii.info_docs_Ltr-to-The-Secretary-General-UN.pdf]

61. "The Rule of Law Trumps the Resort to Violence." 9-9-15
[https://aliejamesllc.files.wordpress.com/2015/04/letter-to-governor-ige-post-supreme-courtpdf.pdf]

62. "King's Message to the Kingdom of Hawai'i". 9-27-14
[https://kingdomofhawaiiinfo.wordpress.com/2014/09/27/kings-message-to-the-kingdom-of-hawaii-9-27-14/]

63. "The Letters to the Hawaiian Governor Ige from King Keli'i Silva, Jr. on the Kingdom of Hawai'i Blog".
[https://kingdomofhawaiiinfo.wordpress.com/?s=ige]

64. "Watching the Hawks RT - Hawaiians Block Construction of Massive Mauna Kea Telescope". 4-21-15
[https://www.youtube.com/watch?v=PE3r4MRim9k]

65. "Lanny Sinkin's Facebook Page."
[https://www.facebook.com/lanny.sinkin?fref=ts]

66. "Questions and Answers from the King". 9-2-14
[https://www.scribd.com/doc/238689770/140902-Questions-and-Answers-From-the-King]

67. "Reaffirmation of Independence", dated 4-21-15. [https://kingdomofhawaiiinfo.wordpress.com/2015/04/22/alii-nui-moi-edmund-k-silva-jr-4-21-15-taxes-proclamation/]

68. "The Mana of Hawai'i is Rising" by Lanny Sinkin. 9-26-14 [https://www.scribd.com/doc/243195905/140926-Questions-and-Answers-From-Lanny-Sinkin]

69. "Radio Interview of Ali'i Mana'o Nui Lanny Sinkin". 10-26-14 [https://kauilapele.wordpress.com/2014/10/26/coming-up-monday-and-tuesday-10-27-10-28-discussion-of-kingdom-issues-with-alii-manao-nui-lanny-sinkin-and-chief-justice-jennifer-pawlowski/]

70. Lanny Sinkin's Letter about the Royal Exchange". 3-11-13 [https://www.scribd.com/doc/244581668/Royal-Kupuna-Exchange-Matter-Lanny-Sinkin-Testimony]

71. "Righting a Substantial Wrong". 12-10-14 [https://kingdomofhawaiiinfo.wordpress.com/2014/12/10/alii-nui-moi-edmund-k-silva-jr-12-10-14-kings-message-about-lowering-the-u-s-flag-and-raising-the-hawaiian-kingdom-flag-at-uh-hilo/]

72. "Alie James' books on Amazon". [http://www.amazon.com/Alie-James/e/B006J6F766/?_encoding=UTF8&camp=1789&creative=390957&linkCode=ur2&qid=1398894596&sr=1-2-ent&tag=alijamhomdect-20&linkId=TIH2JAZHJBIYQFHU]

73. Kauilapele's Blog, the Kingdom Series. [https://kauilapele.wordpress.com/category/hawaiian-kingdom-2/]

74. "Somewhere Over the Rainbow by Israel Kamakawiwo'ole. [https://www.youtube.com/watch?v=w_DKWlrA24k]

75. "Kupuna, Aunty Ipo's 1st Letter of Recognition of the King". 1-17-12 [http://kingdomofhawaii.info/wp-

content/uploads/2015/01/kingdomofhawaii.info_docs_AuntyIpoKahea.pdf]

76. Kupuna, Aunty Ipo's 2nd Letter of Recognition of the King". 1-29-12 [http://kingdomofhawaii.info/wp-content/uploads/2015/01/kingdomofhawaii.info_docs_AuntyIpoandtheKing.pdf]

77. "The Kingdom Path". 9-12-15 [https://kauilapele.wordpress.com/2015/09/16/letter-from-alie-james-9-12-15-the-kingdom-path/]

About the Author

I have many ties to Hawai'i, and have a passion to see the Kingdom of Hawai'i fully restored. Over the last few years, I've told this heartbreaking story numerous times. What I've found is that many people tend to resist the discussion of Hawaiian Sovereignty (Kingdom Restoration). But it is to these very people that I write, and hope will be inspired to embrace the story and pass it on to others.

I have been writing for many years, and have published over 10 books on **Health, Wellness, Natural Beauty, and Anti-Aging.** You can find my books on Amazon Kindle.[72]

I think of myself as a Connector - connecting us to each other; and more importantly, helping us to learn how to connect to our truest self - the Soul and Spirit part of us that seems so hard to reach. This is my writing style, and that is why I have such a passion to see the Kingdom of Hawai'i reconnect to the nations around the world, as the Sovereign Nation of Aloha that she is. I believe that the Kingdom of Hawai'i is the heartbeat of our planet, and is needed more than ever to lead the way.

I invite you to connect with the Kingdom of Hawai'i through the Kingdom of Hawai'i Website,[17] Blog [46] and Facebook Page.[43] In addition to that, you may wish to join the Kingdom's email list: The email address is: lanny.sinkin@gmail.com. You will receive the latest information about the restoration of the Kingdom, as well as the latest letters sent by King Keli'i Silva and Ali'i Mana'o Nui Lanny Sinkin. I, myself, look forward to each and every letter they send out, and I know you will as well.

Coming Soon...
A Sequel to "The Invisible King"

Imagine a paradise on earth. Oh yes, we always think of our favorite vacation spots, but I'm talking about a place where paradise is found more in the heart, rather than in the physical realm. It is a place where the purest of LOVE and RESPECT is the foundation of an entire land of people.

Do you wonder what it would be like to live where peace and harmony among all people is the norm? A place where the land is lush and abundant simply because it is treated with stewardship and respect; treated as a heavenly gift to be cared for, rather than exploited for personal gain.

There once was such a place. You might think I'm referring to the "Garden of Eden", but it is hard to know exactly where and when the Garden of Eden existed. There really was a place - a very long time ago- where the people and land were symbiotic – where both thrived as they cared for one another, and because of this, the people lived in a peaceful, harmonious society. The place... Hawai'i Nei.

Now that you have come to know the "Invisible King", King Edmund Keli'i Silva, Jr., you understand his deep love for Hawai'i Nei. You have read many excerpts from his writings that highlight the depth of his love for the Hawaiian Kingdom, and you've read about his strong desire to see goodness prevail towards all people and living things. You also discovered that his vision for the restored Kingdom includes the Aloha Aina Project and Peace Center.

Recently, I discovered that King Keli'i has much more to share about Kingdom Restoration, especially Hawai'i's spiritual restoration. For this reason, a sequel will be forthcoming.

The King also plans to share his personal perspective of Hawai'i's ancient past, as well as what she became once foreigners arrived, and more importantly, what she will become in the days to come. The King's passion and lifework is now known – he wishes to see the Kingdom of Hawai'i return to a thriving, sustainable land of Aloha- one that is filled with spiritual integrity and a loving spirit.

We, who are Kingdom supporters, believe that Hawai'i will once again become the "heartbeat of the planet" through the efforts of King Keli'i and his Kingdom government. We are excited to participate.

www.ingramcontent.com/pod-product-compliance
Lightning Source LLC
Chambersburg PA
CBHW062109290426
44110CB00023B/2765